THE BIG
TOWER
AIR FRYER

Cookbook For Beginners

800 Days Fresh and Delicious Air Fryer Recipes to Fry, Bake, Grill, and Roast with Your Tower Air Fryer for Whole Year Meals

Winfield Padberg

Warning-Disclaimer

The purpose of this book is to educate and entertain. The author or publisher does not guarantee that anyone following the techniques, suggestions, tips, ideas, or strategies will become successful. The author and publisher shall have neither liability or responsibility to anyone with respect to any loss or damage caused, or alleged to be caused, directly or indirectly by the information contained in this book.

Table of Contents

Chapter 3 Breakfasts

Chapter 4 Fish and Seafood

Chapter 5 Poultry
34

Chapter 7 Vegetables and Sides

56

Chapter 8 Desserts   63

Chapter 9 Staples, Sauces, Dips, and Dressings   70

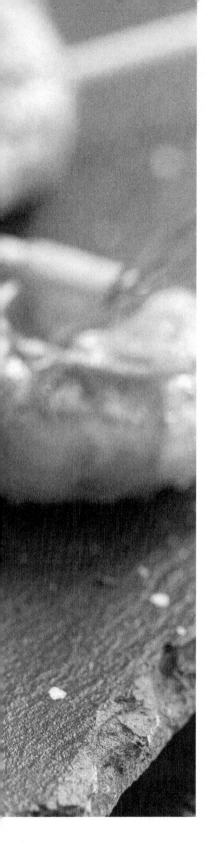

INTRODUCTION

The Air Fryer has been a kitchen appliance favourite so far. It is easy to see why it's really popular, as people love fried foods but are afraid of too much oil, which is just what the air fryer can solve.

The Air Fryer uses convection, which blows hot air all over your food. This simple change ensures that your food is crispy and delicious. It is much healthier because less oil is used compared to a normal fryer. An Air Fryer also takes less time to preheat and make your food compared to a conventional oven.

When I first bought an Air Fryer, I wasn't very convinced that it would work well. But then I was blown away by how easy it was to use, how well it cooked my food and how versatile it was. I was once a person who relied on frozen foods, but now I was making sesame chicken from scratch using my Air Fryer. I have never had to worry about my food being undercooked as it has came out perfect every time.

My experience with the Air Fryer has inspired me to write a book of my favourite recipes. Some of these recipes may be familiar to you. For example, I can teach you how to cook perfectly crispy homemade fries from scratch. Other recipes are more adventurous. However, don't feel intimidated as they are very simple to follow and use everyday ingredients that you can get from your local store. These recipes will taste amazing and can feed a whole family. So why not give them a try!

Chapter 1 Know About the Tower Air Fryer

The Tower Air Fryer is one of the simplest devices to use. All you have to do is plug the Air Fryer into a mains socket and switch it on. After that you put the food you want to cook into the basket. Then choose the temperature that your food needs to be cooked at and set the timer. The Air Fryer will automatically switch off when the timer is up. Your food will come out perfectly cooked, crispy and succulent.

How Does the Air Fryer Work?

The Air Fryer is powered by electricity from your house's electricity supply, which can save 50% on your energy bills. Using vortex technology, rapid circulation is created by a fan to create crispier textures and be 30% faster than a conventional oven. When you set the timer, the Air Fryer automatically turns on and begins to preheat. The fan creates hot air that rushes down and around the food. This rapid circulation makes the food crisp and evenly cooked without using oil. This allows you to cook fried food that will be low in fat.

Five Features of the Tower Air Fryer

Less Fat

The Tower Air Fryer ensures that meals have less fat in them. Oil is very high in fat and when using the Air Fryer, no oil is needed. You still get the same taste and crispiness just with less fat content. This is because the Air Fryer cooks food by using hot air with fine oil droplets. This means the food absorbs much less oil comparing to deep frying. The food cooked in the Air Fryer will have 99% less fat in it.

Faster Cooking Time

Everyone would love to be able to cook their food faster. Using the Tower Air Fryer allows you to cook food in a shorter amount of time. Chips can be cooked as fast as 20 minutes when using the Air Fryer. This is because the heat, which is produced by the air fryer, surrounds the food and cooks it from all angles. Using the Air Fryer cooks food 30% faster than normal.

More Different Types of Meals

You may struggle to create a variety of different meals from home if you don't have the correct kitchen appliances. Using an Air Fryer allows you to have many more meal choices due to it's great functions. It has fry, grill, roast and bake functions that allows you to change up your meals for you and your family. The Tower Air Fryer can cook meals such as stuffed vegetables, muffins, pork chops and much more.

Less Energy Usage

Energy prices are extremely high at the moment and reducing your energy bills is very important for most people. Using the Tower Air Fryer uses up to 50% less energy when cooking. The Air Fryer uses less power than conventional ovens and cooks food 30% faster. It is only 1500w which is much lower than an electric oven, therefore it uses less energy when cooking the same meal.

Large Capacity

Lastly, it can be hard to cook a big meal for your whole family just using one pan. This can be a pain because it means you have to use more kitchen equipment resulting in more time and washing up. The Tower Air Fryer has enough capacity to serve up multiple portions for the whole family to enjoy. It also means that you only have one kitchen appliance to wash up.

Tower Air Fryer Cooking Tips

Preparing for Use

1. If you haven't used your Air Fryer before, follow the manufacturer's instructions for first time use. This involves running the machine empty for a short period of time to eliminate any factory odours.

2. Always preheat the Air Fryer to the recipe temperature before putting the ingredients into the basket. This ensures the food heats up, reducing the chance of food poisoning.

3. For foods that tend to stick, such as burgers and chicken breasts, it is worth oiling the grill of the basket with a pastry brush before use. Lightly brushing the food with oil as well will ensure that the food doesn't stick during cooking. This makes the presentation of the food better and cleaning the basket easier.

Air Frying

1. Do not overfill the Air Fryer basket. The Air Fryer is design requires that hot air is free to circulate around the food to cook it and brown it. If the basket is too full or the food is too compacted only the outer surfaces will cook and potentially leave the inside raw.

2. Don't use too much oil as it is not necessary. The food will still have flavour and be crispy because the rapidly circulating air does this for you. Either use a pastry brush or an oil spray to coat your ingredients before cooking. This will be more than enough oil to brown and crisp the food. Using less oil reduces cooking smells and of course, calories.

3. When cooking moist ingredients such as vegetables, pat them dry before coating them with oil. If there is too much moisture in the Air Fryer, the ingredients will steam instead of roasting which will give them a different flavour to the one intended.

4. Depending on the food, you may need to turn them over halfway through the cooing time. It allows your food to cook evenly and brown all the way round just like you cooked it on the grill or pan.

5. Make sure to shake the Air Fryer a few times when cooking certain foods. This ensures that your ingredients are distributed evenly do that they can cook and brown correctly.

Settings

Temperature: this refers to the degree of heat you need to cook your food. Different foods require different levels of heat. Air Fryers have a dial you use to set the correct temperature. Their manuals also user contain a temperature table that will help you determine the amount of heat you need for the meal your cooking.

Timer: this is the other major setting on the Air Fryer. With the timer, you can tell the appliance how long it should cook for. Be careful to get the appropriate duration for what your cooking from the manual or your cookbook.

Cleaning and Care

Cleaning and taking care of the Tower Air Fryer is essential for all foods to cooks correctly and for the fryer to last as long as possible without breaking. When cleaning the drawer and non-stick basket, don't use metal kitchen utensils or abrasive cleaning materials as this may damage the non-stick coating. Remove the mains socket and let the appliance cool down before cleaning. Wipe the outside of the appliance with a moist cloth. Clean the drawer, separator and basket with hot-water, washing up liquid and a non-abrasive sponge. Clean the inside of the appliance with hot water and a non-abrasive sponge. Clean the heating element with a cleaning brush to remove any food residues.

Chapter 2 Snacks and Appetizers

Bacon-Wrapped Shrimp and Jalapeño

Prep time: 20 minutes | Cook time: 26 minutes | Serves 8

24 large shrimp, peeled and deveined, about 340 g
5 tablespoons barbecue sauce, divided
12 strips bacon, cut in half
24 small pickled jalapeño slices

1. Toss together the shrimp and 3 tablespoons of the barbecue sauce. Let stand for 15 minutes. Soak 24 wooden toothpicks in water for 10 minutes. Wrap 1 piece bacon around the shrimp and jalapeño slice, then secure with a toothpick. 2. Preheat the air fryer to 176°C. 3. Working in batches, place half of the shrimp in the air fryer basket, spacing them ½ inch apart. Air fry for 10 minutes. Turn shrimp over with tongs and air fry for 3 minutes more, or until bacon is golden brown and shrimp are cooked through. 4. Brush with the remaining barbecue sauce and serve.

Crispy Green Bean Fries with Lemon-Yoghurt Sauce

Prep time: 5 minutes | Cook time: 5 minutes | Serves 4

Green Beans:
1 egg
2 tablespoons water
1 tablespoon wholemeal flour
¼ teaspoon paprika
½ teaspoon garlic powder
½ teaspoon salt
60 ml wholemeal breadcrumbs
227 g whole green beans
Lemon-Yoghurt Sauce:
120 ml non-fat plain Greek yoghurt
1 tablespoon lemon juice
¼ teaspoon salt
⅛ teaspoon cayenne pepper

Make the Green Beans: 1. Preheat the air fryer to 192°C. 2. In a medium shallow bowl, beat together the egg and water until frothy. 3. In a separate medium shallow bowl, whisk together the flour, paprika, garlic powder, and salt, then mix in the breadcrumbs. 4. Spray the bottom of the air fryer with cooking spray. 5. Dip each green bean into the egg mixture, then into the bread crumb mixture, coating the outside with the crumbs. Place the green beans in a single layer in the bottom of the air fryer basket. 6. Fry in the air fryer for 5 minutes, or until the breading is golden brown. Make the Lemon-Yoghurt Sauce: 7. In a small bowl, combine the yoghurt, lemon juice, salt, and cayenne. 8. Serve the green bean fries alongside the lemon-yoghurt sauce as a snack or appetizer.

Shishito Peppers with Herb Dressing

Prep time: 10 minutes | Cook time: 6 minutes |
Serves 2 to 4

170 g shishito or Padron peppers
1 tablespoon vegetable oil
Rock salt and freshly ground black pepper, to taste
120 ml mayonnaise
2 tablespoons finely chopped fresh basil leaves
2 tablespoons finely chopped
fresh flat-leaf parsley
1 tablespoon finely chopped fresh tarragon
1 tablespoon finely chopped fresh chives
Finely grated zest of ½ lemon
1 tablespoon fresh lemon juice
Flaky sea salt, for serving

1. Preheat the air fryer to 204°C. 2. In a bowl, toss together the shishitos and oil to evenly coat and season with rock salt and black pepper. Transfer to the air fryer and air fry for 6 minutes, shaking the basket halfway through, or until the shishitos are blistered and lightly charred. 3. Meanwhile, in a small bowl, whisk together the mayonnaise, basil, parsley, tarragon, chives, lemon zest, and lemon juice. 4. Pile the peppers on a plate, sprinkle with flaky sea salt, and serve hot with the dressing.

Rosemary-Garlic Shoestring Fries

Prep time: 5 minutes | Cook time: 18 minutes | Serves 2

1 large russet or Maris Piper potato (about 340 g), scrubbed clean, and julienned
1 tablespoon vegetable oil
Leaves from 1 sprig fresh
rosemary
Rock salt and freshly ground black pepper, to taste
1 garlic clove, thinly sliced
Flaky sea salt, for serving

1. Preheat the air fryer to 204°C. 2. Place the julienned potatoes in a large colander and rinse under cold running water until the water runs clear. Spread the potatoes out on a double-thick layer of paper towels and pat dry. 3. In a large bowl, combine the potatoes, oil, and rosemary. Season with rock salt and pepper and toss to coat evenly. Place the potatoes in the air fryer and air fry for 18 minutes, shaking the basket every 5 minutes and adding the garlic in the last 5 minutes of cooking, or until the fries are golden brown and crisp. 4. Transfer the fries to a plate and sprinkle with flaky sea salt while they're hot. Serve immediately.

Kale Chips with Sesame

Prep time: 15 minutes | Cook time: 8 minutes |
Serves 5

2 L deribbed kale leaves, torn into 2-inch pieces	¼ teaspoon garlic powder
1½ tablespoons olive oil	½ teaspoon paprika
¾ teaspoon chilli powder	2 teaspoons sesame seeds

1. Preheat air fryer to 176°C. 2. In a large bowl, toss the kale with the olive oil, chilli powder, garlic powder, paprika, and sesame seeds until well coated. 3. Put the kale in the air fryer basket and air fry for 8 minutes, flipping the kale twice during cooking, or until the kale is crispy. 4. Serve warm.

Carrot Chips

Prep time: 15 minutes | Cook time: 8 to 10 minutes |
Serves 4

1 tablespoon olive oil, plus more for greasing the basket	and thinly sliced
4 to 5 medium carrots, trimmed	1 teaspoon seasoned salt

1. Preheat the air fryer to 200°C. Grease the air fryer basket with the olive oil. 2. Toss the carrot slices with 1 tablespoon of olive oil and salt in a medium bowl until thoroughly coated. 3. Arrange the carrot slices in the greased basket. You may need to work in batches to avoid overcrowding. 4. Air fry for 8 to 10 minutes until the carrot slices are crisp-tender. Shake the basket once during cooking. 5. Transfer the carrot slices to a bowl and repeat with the remaining carrots. 6. Allow to cool for 5 minutes and serve.

Tangy Fried Pickle Spears

Prep time: 5 minutes | Cook time: 15 minutes |
Serves 6

2 jars sweet and sour pickle spears, patted dry	1 teaspoon sea salt
2 medium-sized eggs	½ teaspoon shallot powder
80 ml milk	⅓ teaspoon chilli powder
1 teaspoon garlic powder	80 ml plain flour
	Cooking spray

1. Preheat the air fryer to 196°C. Spritz the air fryer basket with cooking spray. 2. In a bowl, beat together the eggs with milk. In another bowl, combine garlic powder, sea salt, shallot powder, chilli powder and plain flour until well blended. 3. One by one, roll the pickle spears in the powder mixture, then dredge them in the egg mixture. Dip them in the powder mixture a second time for additional coating. 4. Arrange the coated pickles in the prepared basket. Air fry for 15 minutes until golden and crispy, shaking the basket halfway through to ensure even cooking. 5. Transfer to a plate and let cool for 5 minutes before serving.

Easy Spiced Nuts

Prep time: 5 minutes | Cook time: 25 minutes |
Makes 3 L

1 egg white, lightly beaten	¼ teaspoon ground allspice
60 ml sugar	Pinch ground cayenne pepper
1 teaspoon salt	240 ml pecan halves
½ teaspoon ground cinnamon	240 ml cashews
¼ teaspoon ground cloves	240 ml almonds

1. Combine the egg white with the sugar and spices in a bowl. 2. Preheat the air fryer to 148°C. 3. Spray or brush the air fryer basket with vegetable oil. Toss the nuts together in the spiced egg white and transfer the nuts to the air fryer basket. 4. Air fry for 25 minutes, stirring the nuts in the basket a few times during the cooking process. Taste the nuts (carefully because they will be very hot) to see if they are crunchy and nicely toasted. Air fry for a few more minutes if necessary. 5. Serve warm or cool to room temperature and store in an airtight container for up to two weeks.

Chilli-Brined Fried Calamari

Prep time: 20 minutes | Cook time: 8 minutes | Serves 2

1 (227 g) jar sweet or hot pickled cherry peppers	black pepper, to taste
227 g calamari bodies and tentacles, bodies cut into ½-inch-wide rings	3 large eggs, lightly beaten
	Cooking spray
1 lemon	120 ml mayonnaise
475 ml plain flour	1 teaspoon finely chopped rosemary
Rock salt and freshly ground	1 garlic clove, minced

1. Drain the pickled pepper brine into a large bowl and tear the peppers into bite-size strips. Add the pepper strips and calamari to the brine and let stand in the refrigerator for 20 minutes or up to 2 hours. 2. Grate the lemon zest into a large bowl then whisk in the flour and season with salt and pepper. Dip the calamari and pepper strips in the egg, then toss them in the flour mixture until fully coated. Spray the calamari and peppers liberally with cooking spray, then transfer half to the air fryer. Air fry at 204°C, shaking the basket halfway into cooking, until the calamari is cooked through and golden brown, about 8 minutes. Transfer to a plate and repeat with the remaining pieces. 3. In a small bowl, whisk together the mayonnaise, rosemary, and garlic. Squeeze half the zested lemon to get 1 tablespoon of juice and stir it into the sauce. Season with salt and pepper. Cut the remaining zested lemon half into 4 small wedges and serve alongside the calamari, peppers, and sauce.

Spicy Chicken Bites

Prep time: 10 minutes | Cook time: 10 to 12 minutes | Makes 30 bites

227 g boneless and skinless chicken thighs, cut into 30 pieces

¼ teaspoon rock salt
2 tablespoons hot sauce
Cooking spray

1. Preheat the air fryer to 200ºC. 2. Spray the air fryer basket with cooking spray and season the chicken bites with the rock salt, then place in the basket and air fry for 10 to 12 minutes or until crispy. 3. While the chicken bites cook, pour the hot sauce into a large bowl. 4. Remove the bites and add to the sauce bowl, tossing to coat. Serve warm.

Red Pepper Tapenade

Prep time: 5 minutes | Cook time: 5 minutes | Serves 4

1 large red pepper
2 tablespoons plus 1 teaspoon olive oil, divided
120 ml Kalamata olives, pitted

and roughly chopped
1 garlic clove, minced
½ teaspoon dried oregano
1 tablespoon lemon juice

1. Preheat the air fryer to 192ºC. 2. Brush the outside of a whole red pepper with 1 teaspoon olive oil and place it inside the air fryer basket. Roast for 5 minutes. 3. Meanwhile, in a medium bowl combine the remaining 2 tablespoons of olive oil with the olives, garlic, oregano, and lemon juice. 4. Remove the red pepper from the air fryer, then gently slice off the stem and remove the seeds. Roughly chop the roasted pepper into small pieces. 5. Add the red pepper to the olive mixture and stir all together until combined. 6. Serve with pitta chips, crackers, or crusty bread.

Baked Spanakopita Dip

Prep time: 10 minutes | Cook time: 15 minutes | Serves 2

Olive oil cooking spray
3 tablespoons olive oil, divided
2 tablespoons minced white onion
2 garlic cloves, minced
1 L fresh spinach
113 g soft white cheese, softened

113 g feta cheese, divided
Zest of 1 lemon
¼ teaspoon ground nutmeg
1 teaspoon dried dill
½ teaspoon salt
Pitta chips, carrot sticks, or sliced bread for serving (optional)

1. Preheat the air fryer to 182ºC. Coat the inside of a 6-inch ramekin or baking dish with olive oil cooking spray. 2. In a large skillet over medium heat, heat 1 tablespoon of the olive oil. Add the onion, then cook for 1 minute. 3. Add in the garlic and cook, stirring for 1 minute more. 4. Reduce the heat to low and mix in the spinach and water. Let this cook for 2 to 3 minutes, or until the spinach has wilted. Remove the skillet from the heat. 5. In a medium bowl, combine the soft white cheese, 57 g of the feta, and the remaining 2 tablespoons of olive oil, along with the lemon zest, nutmeg, dill, and salt. Mix until just combined. 6. Add the vegetables to the cheese base and stir until combined. 7. Pour the dip mixture into the prepared ramekin and top with the remaining 57 g of feta cheese. 8. Place the dip into the air fryer basket and cook for 10 minutes, or until heated through and bubbling. 9. Serve with pitta chips, carrot sticks, or sliced bread.

Easy Roasted Chickpeas

Prep time: 5 minutes | Cook time: 15 minutes | Makes about 240 ml

1 (425 g) can chickpeas, drained
2 teaspoons curry powder

¼ teaspoon salt
1 tablespoon olive oil

1. Drain chickpeas thoroughly and spread in a single layer on paper towels. Cover with another paper towel and press gently to remove extra moisture. Don't press too hard or you'll crush the chickpeas. 2. Mix curry powder and salt together. 3. Place chickpeas in a medium bowl and sprinkle with seasonings. Stir well to coat. 4. Add olive oil and stir again to distribute oil. 5. Air fry at 200ºC for 15 minutes, stopping to shake basket about halfway through cooking time. 6. Cool completely and store in airtight container.

Caramelized Onion Dip with White Cheese

Prep time: 5 minutes | Cook time: 30 minutes | Serves 8 to 10

1 tablespoon butter
1 medium onion, halved and thinly sliced
¼ teaspoon rock salt, plus additional for seasoning
113 g soft white cheese
120 ml sour cream

¼ teaspoon onion powder
1 tablespoon chopped fresh chives
Black pepper, to taste
Thick-cut potato crisps or vegetable crisps

1. Place the butter in a baking pan. Place the pan in the air fryer basket. Set the air fryer to 92ºC for 1 minute, or until the butter is melted. Add the onions and salt to the pan. 2. Set the air fryer to 92ºC for 15 minutes, or until onions are softened. Set the air fryer to 192ºC for 15 minutes, until onions are a deep golden brown, stirring two or three times during the cooking time. Let cool completely. 3. In a medium bowl, stir together the cooked onions, soft white cheese, sour cream, onion powder, and chives. Season with salt and pepper. Cover and refrigerate for 2 hours to allow the flavours to blend. 4. Serve the dip with potato crisps or vegetable crisps.

Roasted Grape Dip

Prep time: 10 minutes | Cook time: 8 to 12 minutes | Serves 6

475 ml seedless red grapes, rinsed and patted dry
1 tablespoon apple cider vinegar
1 tablespoon honey
240 ml low-fat Greek yoghurt
2 tablespoons semi-skimmed milk
2 tablespoons minced fresh basil

1. In the air fryer basket, sprinkle the grapes with the cider vinegar and drizzle with the honey. Toss to coat. Roast the grapes at 192°C for 8 to 12 minutes, or until shrivelled but still soft. Remove from the air fryer. 2. In a medium bowl, stir together the yoghurt and milk. 3. Gently blend in the grapes and basil. Serve immediately or cover and chill for 1 to 2 hours.

Goat Cheese and Garlic Crostini

Prep time: 3 minutes | Cook time: 5 minutes | Serves 4

1 wholemeal baguette
60 ml olive oil
2 garlic cloves, minced
113 g goat cheese
2 tablespoons fresh basil, minced

1. Preheat the air fryer to 192°C. 2. Cut the baguette into ½-inch-thick slices. 3. In a small bowl, mix together the olive oil and garlic, then brush it over one side of each slice of bread. 4. Place the olive-oil-coated bread in a single layer in the air fryer basket and bake for 5 minutes. 5. Meanwhile, in a small bowl, mix together the goat cheese and basil. 6. Remove the toast from the air fryer, then spread a thin layer of the goat cheese mixture over the top of each piece and serve.

Dark Chocolate and Cranberry Granola Bars

Prep time: 5 minutes | Cook time: 15 minutes | Serves 6

475 ml certified gluten-free quick oats
2 tablespoons sugar-free dark chocolate chunks
2 tablespoons unsweetened dried cranberries
3 tablespoons unsweetened shredded coconut
120 ml raw honey
1 teaspoon ground cinnamon
⅛ teaspoon salt
2 tablespoons olive oil

1. Preheat the air fryer to 182°C. Line an 8-by-8-inch baking dish with parchment paper that comes up the side so you can lift it out after cooking. 2. In a large bowl, mix together all of the ingredients until well combined. 3. Press the oat mixture into the pan in an even layer. 4. Place the pan into the air fryer basket and bake for 15 minutes. 5. Remove the pan from the air fryer and lift the granola cake out of the pan using the edges of the parchment paper. 6. Allow to cool for 5 minutes before slicing into 6 equal bars. 7. Serve immediately or wrap in plastic wrap and store at room temperature for up to 1 week.

Rumaki

Prep time: 30 minutes | Cook time: 10 to 12 minutes per batch | Makes about 24 rumaki

283 g raw chicken livers
1 can sliced water chestnuts, drained
60 ml low-salt teriyaki sauce
12 slices turkey bacon

1. Cut livers into 1½-inch pieces, trimming out tough veins as you slice. 2. Place livers, water chestnuts, and teriyaki sauce in small container with lid. If needed, add another tablespoon of teriyaki sauce to make sure livers are covered. Refrigerate for 1 hour. 3. When ready to cook, cut bacon slices in half crosswise. 4. Wrap 1 piece of liver and 1 slice of water chestnut in each bacon strip. Secure with toothpick. 5. When you have wrapped half of the livers, place them in the air fryer basket in a single layer. 6. Air fry at 200°C for 10 to 12 minutes, until liver is done, and bacon is crispy. 7. While first batch cooks, wrap the remaining livers. Repeat step 6 to cook your second batch.

Shrimp Pirogues

Prep time: 15 minutes | Cook time: 4 to 5 minutes | Serves 8

340 g small, peeled, and deveined raw shrimp
85 g soft white cheese, room temperature
2 tablespoons natural yoghurt
1 teaspoon lemon juice
1 teaspoon dried dill weed, crushed
Salt, to taste
4 small hothouse cucumbers, each approximately 6 inches long

1. Pour 4 tablespoons water in bottom of air fryer drawer. 2. Place shrimp in air fryer basket in single layer and air fry at 200°C for 4 to 5 minutes, just until done. Watch carefully because shrimp cooks quickly, and overcooking makes it tough. 3. Chop shrimp into small pieces, no larger than ½ inch. Refrigerate while mixing the remaining ingredients. 4. With a fork, mash and whip the soft white cheese until smooth. 5. Stir in the yoghurt and beat until smooth. Stir in lemon juice, dill weed, and chopped shrimp. 6. Taste for seasoning. If needed, add ¼ to ½ teaspoon salt to suit your taste. 7. Store in refrigerator until serving time. 8. When ready to serve, wash and dry cucumbers and split them lengthwise. Scoop out the seeds and turn cucumbers upside down on paper towels to drain for 10 minutes. 9. Just before filling, wipe centres of cucumbers dry. Spoon the shrimp mixture into the pirogues and cut in half crosswise. Serve immediately.

Garlic Edamame

Prep time: 5 minutes | Cook time: 10 minutes |
Serves 4

Olive oil	¼ teaspoon freshly ground
1 (454 g) bag frozen edamame	black pepper
in pods	½ teaspoon red pepper flakes
½ teaspoon salt	(optional)
½ teaspoon garlic salt	

1. Spray the air fryer basket lightly with olive oil. 2. In a medium bowl, add the frozen edamame and lightly spray with olive oil. Toss to coat. 3. In a small bowl, mix together the salt, garlic salt, black pepper, and red pepper flakes (if using). Add the mixture to the edamame and toss until evenly coated. 4. Place half the edamame in the air fryer basket. Do not overfill the basket. 5. Air fry at 192ºC for 5 minutes. Shake the basket and cook until the edamame is starting to brown and get crispy, 3 to 5 more minutes. 6. Repeat with the remaining edamame and serve immediately.

Beef and Mango Skewers

Prep time: 10 minutes | Cook time: 4 to 7 minutes |
Serves 4

340 g beef sirloin tip, cut into	½ teaspoon dried marjoram
1-inch cubes	Pinch of salt
2 tablespoons balsamic vinegar	Freshly ground black pepper, to
1 tablespoon olive oil	taste
1 tablespoon honey	1 mango

1. Preheat the air fryer to 200ºC. 2. Put the beef cubes in a medium bowl and add the balsamic vinegar, olive oil, honey, marjoram, salt, and pepper. Mix well, then massage the marinade into the beef with your hands. Set aside. 3. To prepare the mango, stand it on end and cut the skin off, using a sharp knife. Then carefully cut around the oval pit to remove the flesh. Cut the mango into 1-inch cubes. 4. Thread metal skewers alternating with three beef cubes and two mango cubes. 5. Roast the skewers in the air fryer basket for 4 to 7 minutes, or until the beef is browned and at least 63ºC. 6. Serve hot.

Lemon Shrimp with Garlic Olive Oil

Prep time: 5 minutes | Cook time: 6 minutes | Serves 4

454 g medium shrimp, cleaned	½ teaspoon salt
and deveined	¼ teaspoon red pepper flakes
60 ml plus 2 tablespoons olive	Lemon wedges, for serving
oil, divided	(optional)
Juice of ½ lemon	Marinara sauce, for dipping
3 garlic cloves, minced and	(optional)
divided	

1. Preheat the air fryer to 192ºC. 2. In a large bowl, combine the shrimp with 2 tablespoons of the olive oil, as well as the lemon juice, ⅓ of the minced garlic, salt, and red pepper flakes. Toss to coat the shrimp well. 3. In a small ramekin, combine the remaining 60 ml of olive oil and the remaining minced garlic. 4. Tear off a 12-by-12-inch sheet of aluminium foil. Pour the shrimp into the centre of the foil, then fold the sides up and crimp the edges so that it forms an aluminium foil bowl that is open on top. Place this packet into the air fryer basket. 5. Roast the shrimp for 4 minutes, then open the air fryer and place the ramekin with oil and garlic in the basket beside the shrimp packet. Cook for 2 more minutes. 6. Transfer the shrimp on a serving plate or platter with the ramekin of garlic olive oil on the side for dipping. You may also serve with lemon wedges and marinara sauce, if desired.

Greens Chips with Curried Yoghurt Sauce

Prep time: 10 minutes | Cook time: 5 to 6 minutes |
Serves 4

240 ml low-fat Greek yoghurt	leaves cut into 2- to 3-inch
1 tablespoon freshly squeezed	pieces
lemon juice	½ bunch chard, stemmed, ribs
1 tablespoon curry powder	removed and discarded, leaves
½ bunch curly kale, stemmed,	cut into 2- to 3-inch pieces
ribs removed and discarded,	1½ teaspoons olive oil

1. In a small bowl, stir together the yoghurt, lemon juice, and curry powder. Set aside. 2. In a large bowl, toss the kale and chard with the olive oil, working the oil into the leaves with your hands. This helps break up the fibres in the leaves so the chips are tender. 3. Air fry the greens in batches at 200ºC for 5 to 6 minutes, until crisp, shaking the basket once during cooking. Serve with the yoghurt sauce.

Air Fryer Popcorn with Garlic Salt

Prep time: 3 minutes | Cook time: 10 minutes | Serves 2

2 tablespoons olive oil	1 teaspoon garlic salt
60 ml popcorn kernels	

1. Preheat the air fryer to 192ºC. 2. Tear a square of aluminium foil the size of the bottom of the air fryer and place into the air fryer. 3. Drizzle olive oil over the top of the foil, and then pour in the popcorn kernels. 4. Roast for 8 to 10 minutes, or until the popcorn stops popping. 5. Transfer the popcorn to a large bowl and sprinkle with garlic salt before serving.

String Bean Fries

Prep time: 15 minutes | Cook time: 5 to 6 minutes |
Serves 4

227 g fresh green beans	¼ teaspoon ground black
2 eggs	pepper
4 teaspoons water	¼ teaspoon mustard powder
120 ml white flour	(optional)
120 ml breadcrumbs	Oil for misting or cooking spray
¼ teaspoon salt	

1. Preheat the air fryer to 182°C. 2. Trim stem ends from green beans, wash, and pat dry. 3. In a shallow dish, beat eggs and water together until well blended. 4. Place flour in a second shallow dish. 5. In a third shallow dish, stir together the breadcrumbs, salt, pepper, and dry mustard if using. 6. Dip each bean in egg mixture, flour, egg mixture again, then breadcrumbs. 7. When you finish coating all the green beans, open air fryer and place them in basket. 8. Cook for 3 minutes. 9. Stop and mist green beans with oil or cooking spray. 10. Cook for 2 to 3 more minutes or until green beans are crispy and nicely browned.

Lemony Endive in Curried Yoghurt

Prep time: 5 minutes | Cook time: 10 minutes |
Serves 6

6 heads endive	1 teaspoon garlic powder
120 ml plain and fat-free	½ teaspoon curry powder
yoghurt	Salt and ground black pepper,
3 tablespoons lemon juice	to taste

1. Wash the endives and slice them in half lengthwise. 2. In a bowl, mix together the yoghurt, lemon juice, garlic powder, curry powder, salt and pepper. 3. Brush the endive halves with the marinade, coating them completely. Allow to sit for at least 30 minutes or up to 24 hours. 4. Preheat the air fryer to 160°C. 5. Put the endives in the air fryer basket and air fry for 10 minutes. 6. Serve hot.

Lebanese Muhammara

Prep time: 15 minutes | Cook time: 15 minutes | Serves 6

2 large red peppers	1 teaspoon ground cumin
60 ml plus 2 tablespoons extra-	1 teaspoon rock salt
virgin olive oil	1 teaspoon red pepper flakes
240 ml walnut halves	Raw vegetables (such as
1 tablespoon agave nectar or	cucumber, carrots, courgette
honey	slices, or cauliflower) or toasted
1 teaspoon fresh lemon juice	pitta chips, for serving

1. Drizzle the peppers with 2 tablespoons of the olive oil and place in the air fryer basket. Set the air fryer to 204°C for 10 minutes. 2. Add the walnuts to the basket, arranging them around the peppers. Set the air fryer to 204°C for 5 minutes. 3. Remove the peppers, seal in a resealable plastic bag, and let rest for 5 to 10 minutes. Transfer the walnuts to a plate and set aside to cool. 4. Place the softened peppers, walnuts, agave, lemon juice, cumin, salt, and ½ teaspoon of the pepper flakes in a food processor and purée until smooth. 5. Transfer the dip to a serving bowl and make an indentation in the middle. Pour the remaining 60 ml olive oil into the indentation. Garnish the dip with the remaining ½ teaspoon pepper flakes. 6. Serve with vegetables or toasted pitta chips.

Spinach and Crab Meat Cups

Prep time: 10 minutes | Cook time: 10 minutes |
Makes 30 cups

1 (170 g) can crab meat, drained	¼ teaspoon lemon juice
to yield 80 ml meat	½ teaspoon Worcestershire
60 ml frozen spinach, thawed,	sauce
drained, and chopped	30 mini frozen filo shells,
1 clove garlic, minced	thawed
120 ml grated Parmesan cheese	Cooking spray
3 tablespoons plain yoghurt	

1. Preheat the air fryer to 200°C. 2. Remove any bits of shell that might remain in the crab meat. 3. Mix the crab meat, spinach, garlic, and cheese together. 4. Stir in the yoghurt, lemon juice, and Worcestershire sauce and mix well. 5. Spoon a teaspoon of filling into each filo shell. 6. Spray the air fryer basket with cooking spray and arrange half the shells in the basket. Air fry for 5 minutes. Repeat with the remaining shells. 7. Serve immediately.

Old Bay Chicken Wings

Prep time: 10 minutes | Cook time: 12 to 15 minutes
| Serves 4

2 tablespoons Old Bay or all-	2 teaspoons salt
purpose seasoning	900 g chicken wings, patted dry
2 teaspoons baking powder	Cooking spray

1. Preheat the air fryer to 204°C. Lightly spray the air fryer basket with cooking spray. 2. Combine the seasoning, baking powder, and salt in a large zip-top plastic bag. Add the chicken wings, seal, and shake until the wings are thoroughly coated in the seasoning mixture. 3. Lay the chicken wings in the air fryer basket in a single layer and lightly mist with cooking spray. You may need to work in batches to avoid overcrowding. 4. Air fry for 12 to 15 minutes, flipping the wings halfway through, or until the wings are lightly browned and the internal temperature reaches at least 74°C on a meat thermometer. 5. Remove from the basket to a plate and repeat with the remaining chicken wings. 6. Serve hot.

Homemade Sweet Potato Chips

Prep time: 5 minutes | Cook time: 15 minutes |
Serves 2

1 large sweet potato, sliced thin 2 tablespoons olive oil
⅛ teaspoon salt

1. Preheat the air fryer to 192°C. 2. In a small bowl, toss the sweet potatoes, salt, and olive oil together until the potatoes are well coated. 3. Put the sweet potato slices into the air fryer and spread them out in a single layer. 4. Fry for 10 minutes. Stir, then air fry for 3 to 5 minutes more, or until the chips reach the preferred level of crispiness.

Bacon-Wrapped Pickle Spears

Prep time: 10 minutes | Cook time: 8 minutes |
Serves 4

8 to 12 slices bacon   cheese
60 ml soft white cheese   8 dill pickle spears
60 ml shredded Mozzarella   120 ml ranch dressing

1. Lay the bacon slices on a flat surface. In a medium bowl, combine the soft white cheese and Mozzarella. Stir until well blended. Spread the cheese mixture over the bacon slices. 2. Place a pickle spear on a bacon slice and roll the bacon around the pickle in a spiral, ensuring the pickle is fully covered. (You may need to use more than one slice of bacon per pickle to fully cover the spear.) Tuck in the ends to ensure the bacon stays put. Repeat to wrap all the pickles. 3. Place the wrapped pickles in the air fryer basket in a single layer. Set the air fryer to 204°C for 8 minutes, or until the bacon is cooked through and crisp on the edges. 4. Serve the pickle spears with ranch dressing on the side.

Garlicky and Cheesy French Fries

Prep time: 5 minutes | Cook time: 20 to 25 minutes |
Serves 4

3 medium russet or Maris Piper   80 ml grated Parmesan cheese
potatoes, rinsed, dried, and cut   ½ teaspoon salt
into thin wedges or classic fry   ¼ teaspoon freshly ground
shapes   black pepper
2 tablespoons extra-virgin olive   Cooking oil spray
oil   2 tablespoons finely chopped
1 tablespoon granulated garlic   fresh parsley (optional)

1. In a large bowl combine the potato wedges or fries and the olive oil. Toss to coat. 2. Sprinkle the potatoes with the granulated garlic, Parmesan cheese, salt, and pepper, and toss again. 3. Insert the crisper plate into the basket and the basket into the unit. Preheat the unit by selecting AIR FRY, setting the temperature to 204°C, and setting the time to 3 minutes. Select START/STOP to begin. 4. Once the unit is preheated, spray the crisper plate with cooking oil. Place the potatoes into the basket. 5. Select AIR FRY, set the temperature to 204°C, and set the time to 20 to 25 minutes. Select START/STOP to begin. 6. After about 10 minutes, remove the basket and shake it so the fries at the bottom come up to the top. Reinsert the basket to resume cooking. 7. When the cooking is complete, top the fries with the parsley (if using) and serve hot.

Stuffed Figs with Goat Cheese and Honey

Prep time: 5 minutes | Cook time: 10 minutes |
Serves 4

8 fresh figs   1 tablespoon honey, plus more
57 g goat cheese   for serving
¼ teaspoon ground cinnamon   1 tablespoon olive oil

1. Preheat the air fryer to 182°C. Line an 8-by-8-inch baking dish with parchment paper that comes up the side so you can lift it out after cooking. 2. In a large bowl, mix together all of the ingredients until well combined. 3. Press the oat mixture into the pan in an even layer. 4. Place the pan into the air fryer basket and bake for 15 minutes. 5. Remove the pan from the air fryer and lift the granola cake out of the pan using the edges of the parchment paper. 6. Allow to cool for 5 minutes before slicing into 6 equal bars. 7. Serve immediately or wrap in plastic wrap and store at room temperature for up to 1 week.

Veggie Shrimp Toast

Prep time: 15 minutes | Cook time: 3 to 6 minutes |
Serves 4

8 large raw shrimp, peeled and   1 medium celery stalk, minced
finely chopped   2 tablespoons cornflour
1 egg white   ¼ teaspoon Chinese five-spice
2 garlic cloves, minced   powder
3 tablespoons minced red   3 slices firm thin-sliced no-salt
pepper   wholemeal bread

1. Preheat the air fryer to 176°C. 2. In a small bowl, stir together the shrimp, egg white, garlic, red pepper, celery, cornflour, and five-spice powder. Top each slice of bread with one-third of the shrimp mixture, spreading it evenly to the edges. With a sharp knife, cut each slice of bread into 4 strips. 3. Place the shrimp toasts in the air fryer basket in a single layer. You may need to cook them in batches. Air fry for 3 to 6 minutes, until crisp and golden brown. 4. Serve hot.

Stuffed Fried Mushrooms

Prep time: 20 minutes | Cook time: 10 to 11 minutes | Serves 10

120 ml panko breadcrumbs	1 (227 g) package soft white
½ teaspoon freshly ground	cheese, at room temperature
black pepper	20 cremini or button
½ teaspoon onion powder	mushrooms, stemmed
½ teaspoon cayenne pepper	1 to 2 tablespoons oil

1. In a medium bowl, whisk the breadcrumbs, black pepper, onion powder, and cayenne until blended. 2. Add the soft white cheese and mix until well blended. Fill each mushroom top with 1 teaspoon of the soft white cheese mixture 3. Preheat the air fryer to 182ºC. Line the air fryer basket with a piece of parchment paper. 4. Place the mushrooms on the parchment and spritz with oil. 5. Cook for 5 minutes. Shake the basket and cook for 5 to 6 minutes more until the filling is firm and the mushrooms are soft.

Lemony Pear Chips

Prep time: 15 minutes | Cook time: 9 to 13 minutes | Serves 4

2 firm Bosc or Anjou pears, cut	lemon juice
crosswise into ⅛-inch-thick	½ teaspoon ground cinnamon
slices	⅛ teaspoon ground cardamom
1 tablespoon freshly squeezed	

1. Preheat the air fryer to 192ºC. 2. Separate the smaller stem-end pear rounds from the larger rounds with seeds. Remove the core and seeds from the larger slices. Sprinkle all slices with lemon juice, cinnamon, and cardamom. 3. Put the smaller chips into the air fryer basket. Air fry for 3 to 5 minutes, or until light golden brown, shaking the basket once during cooking. Remove from the air fryer. 4. Repeat with the larger slices, air frying for 6 to 8 minutes, or until light golden brown, shaking the basket once during cooking. 5. Remove the chips from the air fryer. Cool and serve or store in an airtight container at room temperature up for to 2 days.

Crispy Mozzarella Sticks

Prep time: 8 minutes | Cook time: 5 minutes | Serves 4

120 ml plain flour	½ teaspoon garlic salt
1 egg, beaten	6 Mozzarella sticks, halved
120 ml panko breadcrumbs	crosswise
120 ml grated Parmesan cheese	Olive oil spray
1 teaspoon Italian seasoning	

1. Put the flour in a small bowl. 2. Put the beaten egg in another small bowl. 3. In a medium bowl, stir together the panko, Parmesan cheese, Italian seasoning, and garlic salt. 4. Roll a Mozzarella-stick half in the flour, dip it into the egg, and then roll it in the panko mixture to coat. Press the coating lightly to make sure the breadcrumbs stick to the cheese. Repeat with the remaining 11 Mozzarella sticks. 5. Insert the crisper plate into the basket and the basket into the unit. Preheat the unit by selecting AIR FRY, setting the temperature to 204ºC, and setting the time to 3 minutes. Select START/STOP to begin. 6. Once the unit is preheated, spray the crisper plate with olive oil and place a parchment paper liner in the basket. Place the Mozzarella sticks into the basket and lightly spray them with olive oil. 7. Select AIR FRY, set the temperature to 204ºC, and set the time to 5 minutes. Select START/STOP to begin. 8. When the cooking is complete, the Mozzarella sticks should be golden and crispy. Let the sticks stand for 1 minute before transferring them to a serving plate. Serve warm.

Shrimp Toasts with Sesame Seeds

Prep time: 15 minutes | Cook time: 6 to 8 minutes | Serves 4 to 6

230 g raw shrimp, peeled and	1 to 2 teaspoons sriracha sauce
deveined	1 teaspoon soy sauce
1 egg, beaten	½ teaspoon toasted sesame oil
2 spring onions, chopped, plus	6 slices thinly sliced white
more for garnish	sandwich bread
2 tablespoons chopped fresh	120 ml sesame seeds
coriander	Cooking spray
2 teaspoons grated fresh ginger	Thai chilli sauce, for serving

1. Preheat the air fryer to 204ºC. Spritz the air fryer basket with cooking spray. 2. In a food processor, add the shrimp, egg, spring onions, coriander, ginger, sriracha sauce, soy sauce and sesame oil, and pulse until chopped finely. You'll need to stop the food processor occasionally to scrape down the sides. Transfer the shrimp mixture to a bowl. 3. On a clean work surface, cut the crusts off the sandwich bread. Using a brush, generously brush one side of each slice of bread with shrimp mixture. 4. Place the sesame seeds on a plate. Press bread slices, shrimp-side down, into sesame seeds to coat evenly. Cut each slice diagonally into quarters. 5. Spread the coated slices in a single layer in the air fryer basket. 6. Air fry in batches for 6 to 8 minutes, or until golden and crispy. Flip the bread slices halfway through. Repeat with the remaining bread slices. 7. Transfer to a plate and let cool for 5 minutes. Top with the chopped spring onions and serve warm with Thai chilli sauce.

Root Veggie Chips with Herb Salt

Prep time: 10 minutes | Cook time: 8 minutes | Serves 2

1 parsnip, washed
1 small beetroot, washed
1 small turnip, washed
½ small sweet potato, washed
1 teaspoon olive oil

Cooking spray
Herb Salt:
¼ teaspoon rock salt
2 teaspoons finely chopped fresh parsley

1. Preheat the air fryer to 182°C. 2. Peel and thinly slice the parsnip, beetroot, turnip, and sweet potato, then place the vegetables in a large bowl, add the olive oil, and toss. 3. Spray the air fryer basket with cooking spray, then place the vegetables in the basket and air fry for 8 minutes, gently shaking the basket halfway through. 4. While the chips cook, make the herb salt in a small bowl by combining the rock salt and parsley. 5. Remove the chips and place on a serving plate, then sprinkle the herb salt on top and allow to cool for 2 to 3 minutes before serving.

Vegetable Pot Stickers

Prep time: 12 minutes | Cook time: 11 to 18 minutes | Makes 12 pot stickers

240 ml shredded red cabbage
60 ml chopped button mushrooms
60 ml grated carrot
2 tablespoons minced onion

2 garlic cloves, minced
2 teaspoons grated fresh ginger
12 gyoza/pot sticker wrappers
2½ teaspoons olive oil, divided

1. In a baking pan, combine the red cabbage, mushrooms, carrot, onion, garlic, and ginger. Add 1 tablespoon of water. Place in the air fryer and air fry at 188°C for 3 to 6 minutes, until the vegetables are crisp-tender. Drain and set aside. 2. Working one at a time, place the pot sticker wrappers on a work surface. Top each wrapper with a scant 1 tablespoon of the filling. Fold half of the wrapper over the other half to form a half circle. Dab one edge with water and press both edges together. 3. To another pan, add 1¼ teaspoons of olive oil. Put half of the pot stickers, seam-side up, in the pan. Air fry for 5 minutes, or until the bottoms are light golden brown. Add 1 tablespoon of water and return the pan to the air fryer. 4. Air fry for 4 to 6 minutes more, or until hot. Repeat with the remaining pot stickers, remaining 1¼ teaspoons of oil, and another tablespoon of water. Serve immediately.

Chapter 3 Breakfasts

Easy Sausage Pizza

Prep time: 10 minutes | Cook time: 6 minutes | Serves 4

2 tablespoons ketchup
1 pitta bread
80 ml sausage meat

230 g Mozzarella cheese
1 teaspoon garlic powder
1 tablespoon olive oil

1. Preheat the air fryer to 172°C. 2. Spread the ketchup over the pitta bread. 3. Top with the sausage meat and cheese. Sprinkle with the garlic powder and olive oil. 4. Put the pizza in the air fryer basket and bake for 6 minutes. 5. Serve warm.

Double-Dipped Mini Cinnamon Biscuits

Prep time: 15 minutes | Cook time: 13 minutes | Makes 8 biscuits

475 ml blanched almond flour
120 ml liquid or powdered sweetener
1 teaspoon baking powder
½ teaspoon fine sea salt
60 ml plus 2 tablespoons (¾ stick) very cold unsalted butter
60 ml unsweetened, unflavoured almond milk

1 large egg
1 teaspoon vanilla extract
3 teaspoons ground cinnamon
Glaze:
120 ml powdered sweetener
60 ml double cream or unsweetened, unflavoured almond milk

1. Preheat the air fryer to 176°C. Line a pie pan that fits into your air fryer with parchment paper. 2. In a medium-sized bowl, mix together the almond flour, sweetener (if powdered; do not add liquid sweetener), baking powder, and salt. Cut the butter into ½-inch squares, then use a hand mixer to work the butter into the dry ingredients. When you are done, the mixture should still have chunks of butter. 3. In a small bowl, whisk together the almond milk, egg, and vanilla extract (if using liquid sweetener, add it as well) until blended. Using a fork, stir the wet ingredients into the dry ingredients until large clumps form. Add the cinnamon and use your hands to swirl it into the dough. 4. Form the dough into sixteen 1-inch balls and place them on the prepared pan, spacing them about ½ inch apart. (If you're using a smaller air fryer, work in batches if necessary.) Bake in the air fryer until golden, 10 to 13 minutes. Remove from the air fryer and let cool on the pan for at least 5 minutes. 5. While the biscuits bake, make the glaze: Place the powdered sweetener in a small bowl and slowly stir in the heavy cream with a fork. 6. When the biscuits have cooled somewhat, dip the tops into the glaze, allow it to dry a bit, and then dip again for a thick glaze. 7. Serve warm or at room temperature. Store unglazed biscuits in an airtight container in the refrigerator for up to 3 days or in the freezer for up to a month. Reheat in a preheated 176°C air fryer for 5 minutes, or until warmed through, and dip in the glaze as instructed above.

Strawberry Tarts

Prep time: 15 minutes | Cook time: 10 minutes | Serves 6

2 refrigerated piecrusts
120 ml strawberry preserves
1 teaspoon cornflour
Cooking oil spray
120 ml low-fat vanilla yoghurt

30 g cream cheese, at room temperature
3 tablespoons icing sugar
Rainbow sprinkles, for decorating

1. Place the piecrusts on a flat surface. Using a knife or pizza cutter, cut each piecrust into 3 rectangles, for 6 total. Discard any unused dough from the piecrust edges. 2. In a small bowl, stir together the preserves and cornflour. Mix well, ensuring there are no lumps of cornflour remaining. 3. Scoop 1 tablespoon of the strawberry mixture onto the top half of each piece of piecrust. 4. Fold the bottom of each piece up to enclose the filling. Using the back of a fork, press along the edges of each tart to seal. 5. Insert the crisper plate into the basket and the basket into the unit. Preheat the unit by selecting BAKE, setting the temperature to 192°C, and setting the time to 3 minutes. Select START/STOP to begin. 6. Once the unit is preheated, spray the crisper plate with cooking oil. Working in batches, spray the breakfast tarts with cooking oil and place them into the basket in a single layer. Do not stack the tarts. 7. Select BAKE, set the temperature to 192°C, and set the time to 10 minutes. Select START/STOP to begin. 8. When the cooking is complete, the tarts should be light golden brown. Let the breakfast tarts cool fully before removing them from the basket. 9. Repeat steps 5, 6, 7, and 8 for the remaining breakfast tarts. 10. In a small bowl, stir together the yoghurt, cream cheese, and icing sugar. Spread the breakfast tarts with the frosting and top with sprinkles.

Buffalo Chicken Breakfast Muffins

Prep time: 7 minutes | Cook time: 13 to 16 minutes | Serves 10

170 g shredded cooked chicken
85 g blue cheese, crumbled
2 tablespoons unsalted butter, melted
80 ml Buffalo hot sauce, such as Frank's RedHot
1 teaspoon minced garlic
6 large eggs
Sea salt and freshly ground black pepper, to taste
Avocado oil spray

1. In a large bowl, stir together the chicken, blue cheese, melted butter, hot sauce, and garlic. 2. In a medium bowl or large liquid measuring cup, beat the eggs. Season with salt and pepper. 3. Spray 10 silicone muffin cups with oil. Divide the chicken mixture among the cups, and pour the egg mixture over top. 4. Place the cups in the air fryer and set to 150°C. Bake for 13 to 16 minutes, until the muffins are set and cooked through. (Depending on the size of your air fryer, you may need to cook the muffins in batches.)

Berry Muffins

Prep time: 15 minutes | Cook time: 12 to 17 minutes | Makes 8

muffins
315 ml plus 1 tablespoon plain flour, divided
60 ml granulated sugar
2 tablespoons light brown sugar
2 teaspoons baking powder
2 eggs
160 ml whole milk
80 ml neutral oil
235 ml mixed fresh berries

1. In a medium bowl, stir together 315 ml of flour, the granulated sugar, brown sugar, and baking powder until mixed well. 2. In a small bowl, whisk the eggs, milk, and oil until combined. Stir the egg mixture into the dry ingredients just until combined. 3. In another small bowl, toss the mixed berries with the remaining 1 tablespoon of flour until coated. Gently stir the berries into the batter. 4. Double up 16 foil muffin cups to make 8 cups. 5. Insert the crisper plate into the basket and the basket into the unit. Preheat the unit by selecting BAKE, setting the temperature to 156°C, and setting the time to 3 minutes. Select START/STOP to begin. 6. Once the unit is preheated, place 1 L into the basket and fill each three-quarters full with the batter. 7. Select BAKE, set the temperature to 156°C, and set the time for 17 minutes. Select START/STOP to begin. 8. After about 12 minutes, check the muffins. If they spring back when lightly touched with your finger, they are done. If not, resume cooking. 9. When the cooking is done, transfer the muffins to a wire rack to cool. 10. Repeat steps 6, 7, and 8 with the remaining muffin cups and batter. 11. Let the muffins cool for 10 minutes before serving.

Easy Buttermilk Biscuits

Prep time: 5 minutes | Cook time: 18 minutes | Makes 16 biscuits

600 ml plain flour
1 tablespoon baking powder
1 teaspoon coarse or flaky salt
1 teaspoon sugar
½ teaspoon baking soda
8 tablespoons (1 stick) unsalted butter, at room temperature
235 ml buttermilk, chilled

1. Stir together the flour, baking powder, salt, sugar, and baking powder in a large bowl. 2. Add the butter and stir to mix well. Pour in the buttermilk and stir with a rubber spatula just until incorporated. 3. Place the dough onto a lightly floured surface and roll the dough out to a disk, ½ inch thick. Cut out the biscuits with a 2-inch round cutter and re-roll any scraps until you have 16 biscuits. 4. Preheat the air fryer to 164°C. 5. Working in batches, arrange the biscuits in the air fryer basket in a single layer. Bake for about 18 minutes until the biscuits are golden brown. 6. Remove from the basket to a plate and repeat with the remaining biscuits. 7. Serve hot.

Pork Sausage Eggs with Mustard Sauce

Prep time: 20 minutes | Cook time: 12 minutes | Serves 8

450 g pork sausage meat
8 soft-boiled or hard-boiled eggs, peeled
1 large egg
2 tablespoons milk
235 ml crushed pork scratchings
Smoky Mustard Sauce:
60 ml mayonnaise
2 tablespoons sour cream
1 tablespoon Dijon mustard
1 teaspoon chipotle hot sauce

1. Preheat the air fryer to 200°C. 2. Divide the sausage into 8 portions. Take each portion of sausage, pat it down into a patty, and place 1 egg in the middle, gently wrapping the sausage around the egg until the egg is completely covered. (Wet your hands slightly if you find the sausage to be too sticky.) Repeat with the remaining eggs and sausage. 3. In a small shallow bowl, whisk the egg and milk until frothy. In another shallow bowl, place the crushed pork scratchings. Working one at a time, dip a sausage-wrapped egg into the beaten egg and then into the pork scratchings, gently rolling to coat evenly. Repeat with the remaining sausage-wrapped eggs. 4. Arrange the eggs in a single layer in the air fryer basket, and lightly spray with olive oil. Air fry for 10 to 12 minutes, pausing halfway through the baking time to turn the eggs, until the eggs are hot and the sausage is cooked through. 5. To make the sauce: In a small bowl, combine the mayonnaise, sour cream, Dijon, and hot sauce. Whisk until thoroughly combined. Serve with the Scotch eggs.

Egg and Bacon Muffins

Prep time: 5 minutes | Cook time: 15 minutes | Serves 1

2 eggs

Salt and ground black pepper, to taste

1 tablespoon green pesto

85 g shredded Cheddar cheese

140 g cooked bacon

1 spring onion, chopped

1. Preheat the air fryer to 176ºC. Line a cupcake tin with parchment paper. 2. Beat the eggs with pepper, salt, and pesto in a bowl. Mix in the cheese. 3. Pour the eggs into the cupcake tin and top with the bacon and spring onion. 4. Bake in the preheated air fryer for 15 minutes, or until the egg is set. 5. Serve immediately.

Broccoli-Mushroom Frittata

Prep time: 10 minutes | Cook time: 20 minutes | Serves 2

1 tablespoon olive oil

350 ml broccoli florets, finely chopped

120 ml sliced brown mushrooms

60 ml finely chopped onion

½ teaspoon salt

¼ teaspoon freshly ground black pepper

6 eggs

60 ml Parmesan cheese

1. In a nonstick cake pan, combine the olive oil, broccoli, mushrooms, onion, salt, and pepper. Stir until the vegetables are thoroughly coated with oil. Place the cake pan in the air fryer basket and set the air fryer to 204ºC. Air fry for 5 minutes until the vegetables soften. 2. Meanwhile, in a medium bowl, whisk the eggs and Parmesan until thoroughly combined. Pour the egg mixture into the pan and shake gently to distribute the vegetables. Air fry for another 15 minutes until the eggs are set. 3. Remove from the air fryer and let sit for 5 minutes to cool slightly. Use a silicone spatula to gently lift the frittata onto a plate before serving.

Spinach Omelet

Prep time: 5 minutes | Cook time: 12 minutes | Serves 2

4 large eggs

350 ml chopped fresh spinach leaves

2 tablespoons peeled and chopped brown onion

2 tablespoons salted butter, melted

120 ml shredded mild Cheddar cheese

¼ teaspoon salt

1. In an ungreased round nonstick baking dish, whisk eggs. Stir in spinach, onion, butter, Cheddar, and salt. 2. Place dish into air fryer basket. Adjust the temperature to 160ºC and bake for 12 minutes.

Omelet will be done when browned on the top and firm in the middle. 3. Slice in half and serve warm on two medium plates.

Sausage Egg Cup

Prep time: 10 minutes | Cook time: 15 minutes | Serves 6

340 g pork sausage, removed from casings

6 large eggs

½ teaspoon salt

¼ teaspoon ground black pepper

½ teaspoon crushed red pepper flakes

1. Place sausage in six 4-inch ramekins (about 60 g per ramekin) greased with cooking oil. Press sausage down to cover bottom and about ½-inch up the sides of ramekins. Crack one egg into each ramekin and sprinkle evenly with salt, black pepper, and red pepper flakes. 2. Place ramekins into air fryer basket. Adjust the temperature to 176ºC and set the timer for 15 minutes. Egg cups will be done when sausage is fully cooked to at least 64ºC and the egg is firm. Serve warm.

Ham and Cheese Crescents

Prep time: 5 minutes | Cook time: 7 minutes | Makes 8 rolls

Oil, for spraying

1 (230 g) can ready-to-bake croissants

4 slices wafer-thin ham

8 cheese slices

2 tablespoons unsalted butter, melted

1. Line the air fryer basket with parchment and spray lightly with oil. 2. Separate the dough into 8 pieces. 3. Tear the ham slices in half and place 1 piece on each piece of dough. Top each with 1 slice of cheese. 4. Roll up each piece of dough, starting on the wider side. 5. Place the rolls in the prepared basket. Brush with the melted butter. 6. Air fry at 160ºC for 6 to 7 minutes, or until puffed and golden brown and the cheese is melted.

Simple Cinnamon Toasts

Prep time: 5 minutes | Cook time: 4 minutes | Serves 4

1 tablespoon salted butter

2 teaspoons ground cinnamon

4 tablespoons sugar

½ teaspoon vanilla extract

10 bread slices

1. Preheat the air fryer to 192ºC. 2. In a bowl, combine the butter, cinnamon, sugar, and vanilla extract. Spread onto the slices of bread. 3. Put the bread inside the air fryer and bake for 4 minutes or until golden brown. 4. Serve warm.

Spinach and Mushroom Mini Quiche

Prep time: 10 minutes | Cook time: 15 minutes |
Serves 4

1 teaspoon olive oil, plus more for spraying	120 ml shredded Cheddar cheese
235 ml coarsely chopped mushrooms	120 ml shredded Mozzarella cheese
235 ml fresh baby spinach, shredded	¼ teaspoon salt
4 eggs, beaten	¼ teaspoon black pepper

1. Spray 4 silicone baking cups with olive oil and set aside. 2. In a medium sauté pan over medium heat, warm 1 teaspoon of olive oil. Add the mushrooms and sauté until soft, 3 to 4 minutes. 3. Add the spinach and cook until wilted, 1 to 2 minutes. Set aside. 4. In a medium bowl, whisk together the eggs, Cheddar cheese, Mozzarella cheese, salt, and pepper. 5. Gently fold the mushrooms and spinach into the egg mixture. 6. Pour ¼ of the mixture into each silicone baking cup. 7. Place the baking cups into the air fryer basket and air fry at 176°C for 5 minutes. Stir the mixture in each ramekin slightly and air fry until the egg has set, an additional 3 to 5 minutes.

Bacon-and-Eggs Avocado

Prep time: 5 minutes | Cook time: 17 minutes |
Serves 1

1 large egg	Fresh parsley, for serving (optional)
1 avocado, halved, peeled, and pitted	Sea salt flakes, for garnish (optional)
2 slices bacon	

1. Spray the air fryer basket with avocado oil. Preheat the air fryer to 160°C. Fill a small bowl with cool water. 2. Soft-boil the egg: Place the egg in the air fryer basket. Air fry for 6 minutes for a soft yolk or 7 minutes for a cooked yolk. Transfer the egg to the bowl of cool water and let sit for 2 minutes. Peel and set aside. 3. Use a spoon to carve out extra space in the center of the avocado halves until the cavities are big enough to fit the soft-boiled egg. Place the soft-boiled egg in the center of one half of the avocado and replace the other half of the avocado on top, so the avocado appears whole on the outside. 4. Starting at one end of the avocado, wrap the bacon around the avocado to completely cover it. Use toothpicks to hold the bacon in place. 5. Place the bacon-wrapped avocado in the air fryer basket and air fry for 5 minutes. Flip the avocado over and air fry for another 5 minutes, or until the bacon is cooked to your liking. Serve on a bed of fresh parsley, if desired, and sprinkle with salt flakes, if desired. 6. Best served fresh. Store extras in an airtight container in the fridge for up to 4 days. Reheat in a preheated 160°C air fryer for 4 minutes, or until heated through.

Southwestern Ham Egg Cups

Prep time: 5 minutes | Cook time: 12 minutes |
Serves 2

4 (30 g) slices wafer-thin ham	2 tablespoons diced red pepper
4 large eggs	2 tablespoons diced brown onion
2 tablespoons full-fat sour cream	120 ml shredded medium Cheddar cheese
60 ml diced green pepper	

1. Place one slice of ham on the bottom of four baking cups. 2. In a large bowl, whisk eggs with sour cream. Stir in green pepper, red pepper, and onion. 3. Pour the egg mixture into ham-lined baking cups. Top with Cheddar. Place cups into the air fryer basket. 4. Adjust the temperature to 160°C and bake for 12 minutes or until the tops are browned. 5. Serve warm.

Vanilla Granola

Prep time: 5 minutes | Cook time: 40 minutes |
Serves 4

235 ml rolled oats	¼ teaspoon vanilla
3 tablespoons maple syrup	¼ teaspoon cinnamon
1 tablespoon sunflower oil	¼ teaspoon sea salt
1 tablespoon coconut sugar	

1. Preheat the air fryer to 120°C. 2. Mix together the oats, maple syrup, sunflower oil, coconut sugar, vanilla, cinnamon, and sea salt in a medium bowl and stir to combine. Transfer the mixture to a baking pan. 3. Place the pan in the air fryer basket and bake for 40 minutes, or until the granola is mostly dry and lightly browned. Stir the granola four times during cooking. 4. Let the granola stand for 5 to 10 minutes before serving.

Onion Omelette

Prep time: 10 minutes | Cook time: 12 minutes |
Serves 2

3 eggs	1 large onion, chopped
Salt and ground black pepper, to taste	2 tablespoons grated Cheddar cheese
½ teaspoons soy sauce	Cooking spray

1. Preheat the air fryer to 180°C. 2. In a bowl, whisk together the eggs, salt, pepper, and soy sauce. 3. Spritz a small pan with cooking spray. Spread the chopped onion across the bottom of the pan, then transfer the pan to the air fryer. 4. Bake in the preheated air fryer for 6 minutes or until the onion is translucent. 5. Add the egg mixture on top of the onions to coat well. Add the cheese on top, then continue baking for another 6 minutes. 6. Allow to cool before serving.

Breakfast Meatballs

Prep time: 10 minutes | Cook time: 15 minutes |
Makes 18 meatballs

450 g pork sausage meat, removed from casings	120 ml shredded sharp Cheddar cheese
½ teaspoon salt	30 g cream cheese, softened
¼ teaspoon ground black pepper	1 large egg, whisked

1. Combine all ingredients in a large bowl. Form mixture into eighteen 1-inch meatballs. 2. Place meatballs into ungreased air fryer basket. Adjust the temperature to 204ºC and air fry for 15 minutes, shaking basket three times during cooking. Meatballs will be browned on the outside and have an internal temperature of at least 64ºC when completely cooked. Serve warm.

Fried Chicken Wings with Waffles

Prep time: 10 minutes | Cook time: 30 minutes |
Serves 4

8 whole chicken wings	120 ml plain flour
1 teaspoon garlic powder	Cooking oil spray
Chicken seasoning, for preparing the chicken	8 frozen waffles
Freshly ground black pepper, to taste	Pure maple syrup, for serving (optional)

1. In a medium bowl, combine the chicken and garlic powder and season with chicken seasoning and pepper. Toss to coat. 2. Transfer the chicken to a resealable plastic bag and add the flour. Seal the bag and shake it to coat the chicken thoroughly. 3. Insert the crisper plate into the basket and the basket into the unit. Preheat the unit by selecting AIR FRY, setting the temperature to 204ºC, and setting the time to 3 minutes. Select START/STOP to begin. 4. Once the unit is preheated, spray the crisper plate with cooking oil. Using tongs, transfer the chicken from the bag to the basket. It is okay to stack the chicken wings on top of each other. Spray them with cooking oil. 5. Select AIR FRY, set the temperature to 204ºC, and set the time to 20 minutes. Select START/STOP to begin. 6. After 5 minutes, remove the basket and shake the wings. Reinsert the basket to resume cooking. Remove and shake the basket every 5 minutes until the chicken is fully cooked. 7. When the cooking is complete, remove the cooked chicken from the basket; cover to keep warm. 8. Rinse the basket and crisper plate with warm water. Insert them back into the unit. 9. Select AIR FRY, set the temperature to 182ºC, and set the time to 3 minutes. Select START/STOP to begin. 10. Once the unit is preheated, spray the crisper plate with cooking spray. Working in batches, place the frozen waffles into the basket. Do not stack them. Spray the waffles with cooking oil. 11. Select AIR FRY, set the temperature to 182ºC, and set the time to 6 minutes. Select START/STOP to begin. 12. When the cooking is complete, repeat steps 10 and 11 with the remaining waffles. 13. Serve the waffles with the chicken and a touch of maple syrup, if desired.

Lemon-Blueberry Muffins

Prep time: 5 minutes | Cook time: 20 to 25 minutes |
Makes 6

muffins	2 large eggs
300 ml almond flour	3 tablespoons melted butter
3 tablespoons granulated sweetener	1 tablespoon almond milk
1 teaspoon baking powder	1 tablespoon fresh lemon juice
	120 ml fresh blueberries

1. Preheat the air fryer to 176ºC. Lightly coat 6 silicone muffin cups with vegetable oil. Set aside. 2. In a large mixing bowl, combine the almond flour, sweetener, and baking soda. Set aside. 3. In a separate small bowl, whisk together the eggs, butter, milk, and lemon juice. Add the egg mixture to the flour mixture and stir until just combined. Fold in the blueberries and let the batter sit for 5 minutes. 4. Spoon the muffin batter into the muffin cups, about two-thirds full. Air fry for 20 to 25 minutes, or until a toothpick inserted into the center of a muffin comes out clean. 5. Remove the basket from the air fryer and let the muffins cool for about 5 minutes before transferring them to a wire rack to cool completely.

Maple Granola

Prep time: 5 minutes | Cook time: 40 minutes |
Makes 475 ml

235 ml rolled oats	sunflower
3 tablespoons pure maple syrup	¼ teaspoon sea salt
1 tablespoon sugar	¼ teaspoon ground cinnamon
1 tablespoon neutral-flavored oil, such as refined coconut or	¼ teaspoon vanilla extract

1. Insert the crisper plate into the basket and the basket into the unit. Preheat the unit by selecting BAKE, setting the temperature to 120ºC, and setting the time to 3 minutes. Select START/STOP to begin. 2. In a medium bowl, stir together the oats, maple syrup, sugar, oil, salt, cinnamon, and vanilla until thoroughly combined. Transfer the granola to a 6-by-2-inch round baking pan. 3. Once the unit is preheated, place the pan into the basket. 4. Select BAKE, set the temperature to 120ºC and set the time to 40 minutes. Select START/STOP to begin. 5. After 10 minutes, stir the granola well. Resume cooking, stirring the granola every 10 minutes, for a total of 40 minutes, or until the granola is lightly browned and mostly dry. 6. When the cooking is complete, place the granola on a plate to cool. It will become crisp as it cools. Store the completely cooled granola in an airtight container in a cool, dry place for 1 to 2 weeks.

Green Eggs and Ham

Prep time: 5 minutes | Cook time: 10 minutes | Serves 2

1 large Hass avocado, halved and pitted	½ teaspoon fine sea salt
2 thin slices ham	¼ teaspoon ground black pepper
2 large eggs	60 ml shredded Cheddar cheese (omit for dairy-free)
2 tablespoons chopped spring onions, plus more for garnish	

1. Preheat the air fryer to 204ºC. 2. Place a slice of ham into the cavity of each avocado half. Crack an egg on top of the ham, then sprinkle on the green onions, salt, and pepper. 3. Place the avocado halves in the air fryer cut side up and air fry for 10 minutes, or until the egg is cooked to your desired doneness. Top with the cheese (if using) and air fry for 30 seconds more, or until the cheese is melted. Garnish with chopped green onions. 4. Best served fresh. Store extras in an airtight container in the fridge for up to 4 days. Reheat in a preheated 176ºC air fryer for a few minutes, until warmed through.

Hearty Cheddar Biscuits

Prep time: 10 minutes | Cook time: 22 minutes | Makes 8 biscuits

550 ml self-raising flour	plus more to melt on top
2 tablespoons sugar	315 ml buttermilk
120 ml butter, frozen for 15 minutes	235 ml plain flour, for shaping
120 ml grated Cheddar cheese,	1 tablespoon butter, melted

1. Line a buttered 7-inch metal cake pan with parchment paper or a silicone liner. 2. Combine the flour and sugar in a large mixing bowl. Grate the butter into the flour. Add the grated cheese and stir to coat the cheese and butter with flour. Then add the buttermilk and stir just until you can no longer see streaks of flour. The dough should be quite wet. 3. Spread the plain (not self-raising) flour out on a small cookie sheet. With a spoon, scoop 8 evenly sized balls of dough into the flour, making sure they don't touch each other. With floured hands, coat each dough ball with flour and toss them gently from hand to hand to shake off any excess flour. Put each floured dough ball into the prepared pan, right up next to the other. This will help the biscuits rise, rather than spreading out. 4. Preheat the air fryer to 192ºC. 5. Transfer the cake pan to the basket of the air fryer. Let the ends of the aluminum foil sling hang across the cake pan before returning the basket to the air fryer. 6. Air fry for 20 minutes. Check the biscuits twice to make sure they are not getting too brown on top. If they are, re-arrange the aluminum foil strips to cover any brown parts. After 20 minutes, check the biscuits by inserting a toothpick into the center of the biscuits. It should come out clean. If it needs a little more time, continue to air fry for two extra minutes. Brush the tops of the biscuits with some melted butter and sprinkle a little more grated cheese on top if desired. Pop the basket back into the air fryer for another 2 minutes. 7. Remove the cake pan from the air fryer. Let the biscuits cool for just a minute or two and then turn them out onto a plate and pull apart. Serve immediately.

Wholemeal Blueberry Muffins

Prep time: 10 minutes | Cook time: 15 minutes | Serves 6

Olive oil cooking spray	350 ml plus 1 tablespoon wholemeal, divided
120 ml unsweetened applesauce	½ teaspoon baking soda
60 ml honey	½ teaspoon baking powder
120 ml non-fat plain Greek yoghurt	½ teaspoon salt
1 teaspoon vanilla extract	120 ml blueberries, fresh or frozen
1 large egg	

1. Preheat the air fryer to 182ºC. Lightly coat the inside of six silicone muffin cups or a six-cup muffin tin with olive oil cooking spray. 2. In a large bowl, combine the applesauce, honey, yoghurt, vanilla, and egg and mix until smooth. 3. Sift in 350 ml of the flour, the baking soda, baking powder, and salt into the wet mixture, then stir until just combined. 4. In a small bowl, toss the blueberries with the remaining 1 tablespoon flour, then fold the mixture into the muffin batter. 5. Divide the mixture evenly among the prepared muffin cups and place into the basket of the air fryer. Bake for 12 to 15 minutes, or until golden brown on top and a toothpick inserted into the middle of one of the muffins comes out clean. 6. Allow to cool for 5 minutes before serving.

Strawberry Toast

Prep time: 10 minutes | Cook time: 8 minutes | Makes 4 toasts

4 slices bread, ½-inch thick	235 ml sliced strawberries
Butter-flavoured cooking spray	1 teaspoon sugar

1. Spray one side of each bread slice with butter-flavored cooking spray. Lay slices sprayed side down. 2. Divide the strawberries among the bread slices. 3. Sprinkle evenly with the sugar and place in the air fryer basket in a single layer. 4. Air fry at 200ºC for 8 minutes. The bottom should look brown and crisp and the top should look glazed.

Baked Potato Breakfast Boats

Prep time: 10 minutes | Cook time: 20 minutes | Serves 4

2 large white potatoes, scrubbed
Olive oil
Salt and freshly ground black pepper, to taste
4 eggs

2 tablespoons chopped, cooked bacon
235 ml shredded Cheddar cheese

1. Poke holes in the potatoes with a fork and microwave on full power for 5 minutes. 2. Turn potatoes over and cook an additional 3 to 5 minutes, or until the potatoes are fork-tender. 3. Cut the potatoes in half lengthwise and use a spoon to scoop out the inside of the potato. Be careful to leave a layer of potato so that it makes a sturdy "boat." 4. Preheat the air fryer to 176°C. 5. Lightly spray the air fryer basket with olive oil. Spray the skin side of the potatoes with oil and sprinkle with salt and pepper to taste. 6. Place the potato skins in the air fryer basket, skin-side down. Crack one egg into each potato skin. 7. Sprinkle ½ tablespoon of bacon pieces and 60 ml shredded cheese on top of each egg. Sprinkle with salt and pepper to taste. 8. Air fry until the yolk is slightly runny, 5 to 6 minutes, or until the yolk is fully cooked, 7 to 10 minutes.

Meritage Eggs

Prep time: 5 minutes | Cook time: 8 minutes | Serves 2

2 teaspoons unsalted butter (or coconut oil for dairy-free), for greasing the ramekins
4 large eggs
2 teaspoons chopped fresh thyme
½ teaspoon fine sea salt
¼ teaspoon ground black pepper

2 tablespoons double cream (or unsweetened, unflavoured almond milk for dairy-free)
3 tablespoons finely grated Parmesan cheese (or chive cream cheese style spread, softened, for dairy-free)
Fresh thyme leaves, for garnish (optional)

1. Preheat the air fryer to 204°C. Grease two (110 g) ramekins with the butter. 2. Crack 2 eggs into each ramekin and divide the thyme, salt, and pepper between the ramekins. Pour 1 tablespoon of the heavy cream into each ramekin. Sprinkle each ramekin with 1½ tablespoons of the Parmesan cheese. 3. Place the ramekins in the air fryer and bake for 8 minutes for soft-cooked yolks (longer if you desire a harder yolk). 4. Garnish with a sprinkle of ground black pepper and thyme leaves, if desired. Best served fresh.

Apple Rolls

Prep time: 20 minutes | Cook time: 20 to 24 minutes | Makes 12 rolls

Apple Rolls:
475 ml plain flour, plus more for dusting
2 tablespoons granulated sugar
1 teaspoon salt
3 tablespoons butter, at room temperature
180 ml milk, whole or semi-skimmed
120 ml packed light brown

sugar
1 teaspoon ground cinnamon
1 large Granny Smith apple, peeled and diced
1 to 2 tablespoons oil
Icing:
120 ml icing sugar
½ teaspoon vanilla extract
2 to 3 tablespoons milk, whole or semi-skimmed

Make the Apple Rolls 1. In a large bowl, whisk the flour, granulated sugar, and salt until blended. Stir in the butter and milk briefly until a sticky dough forms. 2. In a small bowl, stir together the brown sugar, cinnamon, and apple. 3. Place a piece of parchment paper on a work surface and dust it with flour. Roll the dough on the prepared surface to ¼ inch thickness. 4. Spread the apple mixture over the dough. Roll up the dough jelly roll-style, pinching the ends to seal. Cut the dough into 12 rolls. 5. Preheat the air fryer to 160°C. 6. Line the air fryer basket with parchment paper and spritz it with oil. Place 6 rolls on the prepared parchment. 7. Bake for 5 minutes. Flip the rolls and bake for 5 to 7 minutes more until lightly browned. Repeat with the remaining rolls. Make the Icing 8. In a medium bowl, whisk the icing sugar, vanilla, and milk until blended. 9. Drizzle over the warm rolls.

Bacon Eggs on the Go

Prep time: 5 minutes | Cook time: 15 minutes | Serves 1

2 eggs
110 g bacon, cooked

Salt and ground black pepper, to taste

1. Preheat the air fryer to 204°C. Put liners in a regular cupcake tin. 2. Crack an egg into each of the cups and add the bacon. Season with some pepper and salt. 3. Bake in the preheated air fryer for 15 minutes, or until the eggs are set. Serve warm.

Chapter 4 Fish and Seafood

Tuna and Fruit Kebabs

Prep time: 15 minutes | Cook time: 8 to 12 minutes | Serves 4

455 g tuna steaks, cut into 1-inch cubes
85 g canned pineapple chunks, drained, juice reserved
75 g large red grapes
1 tablespoon honey
2 teaspoons grated fresh ginger
1 teaspoon olive oil
Pinch cayenne pepper

1. Thread the tuna, pineapple, and grapes on 8 bamboo or 4 metal skewers that fit in the air fryer. 2. In a small bowl, whisk the honey, 1 tablespoon of reserved pineapple juice, the ginger, olive oil, and cayenne. Brush this mixture over the kebabs. Let them stand for 10 minutes. 3. Air fry the kebabs at 188°C for 8 to 12 minutes, or until the tuna reaches an internal temperature of at least 64°C on a meat thermometer, and the fruit is tender and glazed, brushing once with the remaining sauce. Discard any remaining marinade. Serve immediately.

Coconut Prawns with Spicy Dipping Sauce

Prep time: 15 minutes | Cook time: 8 minutes | Serves 4

70 g pork scratchings
70 g desiccated, unsweetened coconut
85 g coconut flour
1 teaspoon onion powder
1 teaspoon garlic powder
2 eggs
680 g large prawns, peeled and deveined
½ teaspoon salt
¼ teaspoon freshly ground black pepper
Spicy Dipping Sauce:
115 g mayonnaise
2 tablespoons Sriracha
Zest and juice of ½ lime
1 clove garlic, minced

1. Preheat the air fryer to 200°C. 2. In a food processor fitted with a metal blade, combine the pork scratchings and desiccated coconut. Pulse until the mixture resembles coarse crumbs. Transfer to a shallow bowl. 3. In another shallow bowl, combine the coconut flour, onion powder, and garlic powder; mix until thoroughly combined. 4. In a third shallow bowl, whisk the eggs until slightly frothy. 5. In a large bowl, season the prawns with the salt and pepper, tossing gently to coat. 6. Working a few pieces at a time, dredge the prawns in the flour mixture, followed by the eggs, and finishing with the pork rind crumb mixture. Arrange the prawns on a baking sheet until ready to air fry. 7. Working in batches if necessary, arrange the prawns in a single layer in the air fryer basket. Pausing halfway through the cooking time to turn the prawns, air fry for 8 minutes until cooked through. 8. To make the sauce: In a small bowl, combine the mayonnaise, Sriracha, lime zest and juice, and garlic. Whisk until thoroughly combined. Serve alongside the prawns.

Rainbow Salmon Kebabs

Prep time: 10 minutes | Cook time: 8 minutes | Serves 2

170 g boneless, skinless salmon, cut into 1-inch cubes
¼ medium red onion, peeled and cut into 1-inch pieces
½ medium yellow bell pepper, seeded and cut into 1-inch pieces
½ medium courgette, trimmed and cut into ½-inch slices
1 tablespoon olive oil
½ teaspoon salt
¼ teaspoon ground black pepper

1. Using one (6-inch) skewer, skewer 1 piece salmon, then 1 piece onion, 1 piece bell pepper, and finally 1 piece courgette. Repeat this pattern with additional skewers to make four kebabs total. Drizzle with olive oil and sprinkle with salt and black pepper. 2. Place kebabs into ungreased air fryer basket. Adjust the temperature to 204°C and air fry for 8 minutes, turning kebabs halfway through cooking. Salmon will easily flake and have an internal temperature of at least 64°C when done; vegetables will be tender. Serve warm.

Crab Legs

Prep time: 5 minutes | Cook time: 15 minutes | Serves 4

60 g salted butter, melted and divided
1.4 kg crab legs
¼ teaspoon garlic powder
Juice of ½ medium lemon

1. In a large bowl, drizzle 2 tablespoons butter over crab legs. Place crab legs into the air fryer basket. 2. Adjust the temperature to 204°C and air fry for 15 minutes. 3. Shake the air fryer basket to toss the crab legs halfway through the cooking time. 4. In a small bowl, mix remaining butter, garlic powder, and lemon juice. 5. To serve, crack open crab legs and remove meat. Dip in lemon butter.

Paprika Crab Burgers

Prep time: 30 minutes | Cook time: 14 minutes | Serves 3

2 eggs, beaten	280 g crab meat
1 shallot, chopped	1 teaspoon smoked paprika
2 garlic cloves, crushed	½ teaspoon ground black
1 tablespoon olive oil	pepper
1 teaspoon yellow mustard	Sea salt, to taste
1 teaspoon fresh coriander, chopped	70 g Parmesan cheese

1. In a mixing bowl, thoroughly combine the eggs, shallot, garlic, olive oil, mustard, coriander, crab meat, paprika, black pepper, and salt. Mix until well combined. 2. Shape the mixture into 6 patties. Roll the crab patties over grated Parmesan cheese, coating well on all sides. Place in your refrigerator for 2 hours. 3. Spritz the crab patties with cooking oil on both sides. Cook in the preheated air fryer at 182ºC for 14 minutes. Serve on dinner rolls if desired. Bon appétit!

Panko-Crusted Fish Sticks

Prep time: 10 minutes | Cook time: 15 minutes | Serves 4

Tartar Sauce:	75 g plain flour
470 ml mayonnaise	120 g panko bread crumbs
2 tablespoons dill pickle relish	2 tablespoons Creole seasoning
1 tablespoon dried minced onions	2 teaspoons garlic granules
Fish Sticks:	1 teaspoon onion powder
Olive or vegetable oil, for spraying	½ teaspoon salt
455 g tilapia fillets	¼ teaspoon freshly ground black pepper
	1 large egg

Make the Tartar Sauce: 1. In a small bowl, whisk together the mayonnaise, pickle relish, and onions. Cover with plastic wrap and refrigerate until ready to serve. You can make this sauce ahead of time; the flavors will intensify as it chills. Make the Fish Sticks: 2. Preheat the air fryer to 176ºC. Line the air fryer basket with baking paper and spray lightly with oil. 3. Cut the fillets into equal-size sticks and place them in a zip-top plastic bag. 4. Add the flour to the bag, seal, and shake well until evenly coated. 5. In a shallow bowl, mix together the bread crumbs, Creole seasoning, garlic, onion powder, salt, and black pepper. 6. In a small bowl, whisk the egg. 7. Dip the fish sticks in the egg, then dredge in the bread crumb mixture until completely coated. 8. Place the fish sticks in the prepared basket. You may need to work in batches, depending on the size of your air fryer. Do not overcrowd. Spray lightly with oil. 9. Cook for 12 to 15 minutes, or until browned and cooked through. Serve with the tartar sauce.

Roasted Salmon Fillets

Prep time: 5 minutes | Cook time: 10 minutes | Serves 2

2 (230 g) skin-on salmon fillets, 1½ inches thick	Salt and pepper, to taste
1 teaspoon vegetable oil	Vegetable oil spray

1. Preheat the air fryer to 204ºC. 2. Make foil sling for air fryer basket by folding 1 long sheet of aluminum foil so it is 4 inches wide. Lay sheet of foil widthwise across basket, pressing foil into and up sides of basket. Fold excess foil as needed so that edges of foil are flush with top of basket. Lightly spray foil and basket with vegetable oil spray. 3. Pat salmon dry with paper towels, rub with oil, and season with salt and pepper. Arrange fillets skin side down on sling in prepared basket, spaced evenly apart. Air fry salmon until center is still translucent when checked with the tip of a paring knife and registers 52ºC (for medium-rare), 10 to 14 minutes, using sling to rotate fillets halfway through cooking. 4. Using the sling, carefully remove salmon from air fryer. Slide fish spatula along underside of fillets and transfer to individual serving plates, leaving skin behind. Serve.

Cheesy Tuna Patties

Prep time: 5 minutes | Cook time: 17 to 18 minutes | Serves 4

Tuna Patties:	pepper, to taste
455 g canned tuna, drained	1 tablespoon sesame oil
1 egg, whisked	Cheese Sauce:
2 tablespoons shallots, minced	1 tablespoon butter
1 garlic clove, minced	240 ml beer
1 cup grated Romano cheese	2 tablespoons grated Cheddar
Sea salt and ground black	cheese

1. Mix together the canned tuna, whisked egg, shallots, garlic, cheese, salt, and pepper in a large bowl and stir to incorporate. 2. Divide the tuna mixture into four equal portions and form each portion into a patty with your hands. Refrigerate the patties for 2 hours. 3. When ready, brush both sides of each patty with sesame oil. 4. Preheat the air fryer to 182ºC. 5. Place the patties in the air fryer basket and bake for 14 minutes, flipping the patties halfway through, or until lightly browned and cooked through. 6. Meanwhile, melt the butter in a pan over medium heat. 7. Pour in the beer and whisk constantly, or until it begins to bubble. 8. Add the grated Colby cheese and mix well. Continue cooking for 3 to 4 minutes, or until the cheese melts. Remove the patties from the basket to a plate. Drizzle them with the cheese sauce and serve immediately.

Cilantro Lime Baked Salmon

Prep time: 10 minutes | Cook time: 12 minutes | Serves 2

2 salmon fillets, 85 g each, skin removed	½ teaspoon finely minced garlic
1 tablespoon salted butter, melted	20 g sliced pickled jalapeños
	½ medium lime, juiced
1 teaspoon chilli powder	2 tablespoons chopped coriander

1. Place salmon fillets into a round baking pan. Brush each with butter and sprinkle with chilli powder and garlic. 2. Place jalapeño slices on top and around salmon. Pour half of the lime juice over the salmon and cover with foil. Place pan into the air fryer basket. 3. Adjust the temperature to 188ºC and bake for 12 minutes. 4. When fully cooked, salmon should flake easily with a fork and reach an internal temperature of at least 64ºC. 5. To serve, spritz with remaining lime juice and garnish with coriander.

Lemon Mahi-Mahi

Prep time: 5 minutes | Cook time: 14 minutes | Serves 2

Olive or vegetable oil, for spraying	¼ teaspoon salt
2 (170 g) mahi-mahi fillets	¼ teaspoon freshly ground black pepper
1 tablespoon lemon juice	1 tablespoon chopped fresh dill
1 tablespoon olive oil	2 lemon slices

1. Line the air fryer basket with baking paper and spray lightly with oil. 2. Place the mahi-mahi in the prepared basket. 3. In a small bowl, whisk together the lemon juice and olive oil. Brush the mixture evenly over the mahi-mahi. 4. Sprinkle the mahi-mahi with the salt and black pepper and top with the dill. 5. Air fry at 204ºC for 12 to 14 minutes, depending on the thickness of the fillets, until they flake easily. 6. Transfer to plates, top each with a lemon slice, and serve.

Tortilla Prawn Tacos

Prep time: 10 minutes | Cook time: 6 minutes | Serves 4

Spicy Mayo:	2 tablespoons chopped fresh cilantro
3 tablespoons mayonnaise	
1 tablespoon Louisiana-style hot pepper sauce, or Sriracha	Juice of 1 lime
Coriander-Lime Slaw:	¼ teaspoon kosher salt
180 g shredded green cabbage	Prawns:
½ small red onion, thinly sliced	1 large egg, beaten
1 small jalapeño, thinly sliced	1 cup crushed tortilla chips
	24 jumbo prawns (about 455 g), peeled and deveined
⅛ teaspoon kosher or coarse sea salt	Cooking spray
	8 corn tortillas, for serving

1. For the spicy mayo: In a small bowl, mix the mayonnaise and hot pepper sauce. 2. For the coriander-lime slaw: In a large bowl, toss together the cabbage, onion, jalapeño, coriander, lime juice, and salt to combine. Cover and refrigerate to chill. 3. For the prawns: Place the egg in a shallow bowl and the crushed tortilla chips in another. Season the prawns with the salt. Dip the prawns in the egg, then in the crumbs, pressing gently to adhere. Place on a work surface and spray both sides with oil. 4. Preheat the air fryer to 182ºC. 5. Working in batches, arrange a single layer of the prawns in the air fryer basket. Air fry for 6 minutes, flipping halfway, until golden and cooked through in the center. 6. To serve, place 2 tortillas on each plate and top each with 3 prawns. Top each taco with ¼ of the slaw, then drizzle with spicy mayo.

Fish Taco Bowl

Prep time: 10 minutes | Cook time: 12 minutes | Serves 4

½ teaspoon salt	cabbage
¼ teaspoon garlic powder	735 g mayonnaise
¼ teaspoon ground cumin	¼ teaspoon ground black pepper
4 cod fillets, 110 g each	
360 g finely shredded green	20 g chopped pickled jalapeños

1. Sprinkle salt, garlic powder, and cumin over cod and place into ungreased air fryer basket. Adjust the temperature to 176ºC and air fry for 12 minutes, turning fillets halfway through cooking. Cod will flake easily and have an internal temperature of at least 64ºC when done. 2. In a large bowl, toss cabbage with mayonnaise, pepper, and jalapeños until fully coated. Serve cod warm over cabbage slaw on four medium plates.

Honey-Balsamic Salmon

Prep time: 5 minutes | Cook time: 8 minutes | Serves 2

Olive or vegetable oil, for spraying	2 teaspoons red pepper flakes
	2 teaspoons olive oil
2 (170 g) salmon fillets	½ teaspoon salt
60 ml balsamic vinegar	¼ teaspoon freshly ground black pepper
2 tablespoons honey	

1. Line the air fryer basket with baking paper and spray lightly with oil. 2. Place the salmon in the prepared basket. 3. In a small bowl, whisk together the balsamic vinegar, honey, red pepper flakes, olive oil, salt, and black pepper. Brush the mixture over the salmon. 4. Roast at 200ºC for 7 to 8 minutes, or until the internal temperature reaches 64ºC. Serve immediately.

Tuna Nuggets in Hoisin Sauce

Prep time: 15 minutes | Cook time: 5 to 7 minutes |
Serves 4

120 ml hoisin sauce	½ small onion, quartered and
2 tablespoons rice wine vinegar	thinly sliced
2 teaspoons sesame oil	230 g fresh tuna, cut into 1-inch
1 teaspoon garlic powder	cubes
2 teaspoons dried lemongrass	Cooking spray
¼ teaspoon red pepper flakes	560 g cooked jasmine rice

1. Mix the hoisin sauce, vinegar, sesame oil, and seasonings together. 2. Stir in the onions and tuna nuggets. 3. Spray a baking pan with nonstick spray and pour in tuna mixture. 4. Roast at 200ºC for 3 minutes. Stir gently. 5. Cook 2 minutes and stir again, checking for doneness. Tuna should be barely cooked through, just beginning to flake and still very moist. If necessary, continue cooking and stirring in 1-minute intervals until done. 6. Serve warm over hot jasmine rice.

Bacon-Wrapped Scallops

Prep time: 5 minutes | Cook time: 10 minutes |
Serves 4

8 sea scallops, 30 g each,	¼ teaspoon salt
cleaned and patted dry	¼ teaspoon ground black
8 slices bacon	pepper

1. Wrap each scallop in 1 slice bacon and secure with a toothpick. Sprinkle with salt and pepper. 2. Place scallops into ungreased air fryer basket. Adjust the temperature to 182ºC and air fry for 10 minutes. Scallops will be opaque and firm, and have an internal temperature of 56ºC when done. Serve warm.

Tuna Steaks with Olive Tapenade

Prep time: 10 minutes | Cook time: 10 minutes |
Serves 4

4 (170 g) ahi tuna steaks	1 tablespoon olive oil
1 tablespoon olive oil	1 tablespoon chopped fresh
Salt and freshly ground black	parsley
pepper, to taste	1 clove garlic
½ lemon, sliced into 4 wedges	2 teaspoons red wine vinegar
Olive Tapenade:	1 teaspoon capers, drained
90 g pitted Kalamata olives	

1. Preheat the air fryer to 204ºC. 2. Drizzle the tuna steaks with the olive oil and sprinkle with salt and black pepper. Arrange the tuna steaks in a single layer in the air fryer basket. Pausing to turn the steaks halfway through the cooking time, air fry for 10 minutes until the fish is firm. 3. To make the tapenade: In a food processor fitted with a metal blade, combine the olives, olive oil, parsley, garlic, vinegar, and capers. Pulse until the mixture is finely chopped, pausing to scrape down the sides of the bowl if necessary. Spoon the tapenade over the top of the tuna steaks and serve with lemon wedges.

Almond-Crusted Fish

Prep time: 15 minutes | Cook time: 10 minutes |
Serves 4

4 firm white fish fillets, 110g	Salt and pepper, to taste
each	940 g plain flour
45 g breadcrumbs	1 egg, beaten with 1 tablespoon
20 g slivered almonds, crushed	water
2 tablespoons lemon juice	Olive or vegetable oil for
⅛ teaspoon cayenne	misting or cooking spray

1. Split fish fillets lengthwise down the center to create 8 pieces. 2. Mix breadcrumbs and almonds together and set aside. 3. Mix the lemon juice and cayenne together. Brush on all sides of fish. 4. Season fish to taste with salt and pepper. 5. Place the flour on a sheet of wax paper. 6. Roll fillets in flour, dip in egg wash, and roll in the crumb mixture. 7. Mist both sides of fish with oil or cooking spray. 8. Spray the air fryer basket and lay fillets inside. 9. Roast at 200ºC for 5 minutes, turn fish over, and cook for an additional 5 minutes or until fish is done and flakes easily.

Pecan-Crusted Catfish

Prep time: 5 minutes | Cook time: 12 minutes |
Serves 4

65 g pecans, finely crushed	4 catfish fillets, 110g each
1 teaspoon fine sea salt	For Garnish (Optional):
¼ teaspoon ground black	Fresh oregano
pepper	Pecan halves

1. Spray the air fryer basket with avocado oil. Preheat the air fryer to 192ºC. 2. In a large bowl, mix the crushed pecan, salt, and pepper. One at a time, dredge the catfish fillets in the mixture, coating them well. Use your hands to press the pecan meal into the fillets. Spray the fish with avocado oil and place them in the air fryer basket. 3. Air fry the coated catfish for 12 minutes, or until it flakes easily and is no longer translucent in the center, flipping halfway through. 4. Garnish with oregano sprigs and pecan halves, if desired. 5. Store leftovers in an airtight container in the fridge for up to 3 days. Reheat in a preheated 176ºC air fryer for 4 minutes, or until heated through.

Steamed Tuna with Lemongrass

Prep time: 10 minutes | Cook time: 10 minutes |
Serves 4

4 small tuna steaks	ginger
2 tablespoons low-sodium soy sauce	⅛ teaspoon freshly ground black pepper
2 teaspoons sesame oil	1 stalk lemongrass, bent in half
2 teaspoons rice wine vinegar	3 tablespoons freshly squeezed lemon juice
1 teaspoon grated peeled fresh	

1. Place the tuna steaks on a plate. 2. In a small bowl, whisk the soy sauce, sesame oil, vinegar, and ginger until combined. Pour this mixture over the tuna and gently rub it into both sides. Sprinkle the fish with the pepper. Let marinate for 10 minutes. 3. Insert the crisper plate into the basket and the basket into the unit. Preheat the unit to 200ºC. 4. Once the unit is preheated, place the lemongrass into the basket and top it with the tuna steaks. Drizzle the tuna with the lemon juice and 1 tablespoon of water. 5. Cook for 10 minutes. 6. When the cooking is complete, a food thermometer inserted into the tuna should register at least 64ºC. Discard the lemongrass and serve the tuna.

Cornmeal-Crusted Trout Fingers

Prep time: 15 minutes | Cook time: 6 minutes | Serves 2

70 g yellow cornmeal, medium or finely ground (not coarse)	into strips 1 inch wide and 3 inches long
40 g plain flour	3 large eggs, lightly beaten
1½ teaspoons baking powder	Cooking spray
1 teaspoon kosher or coarse sea salt, plus more as needed	115 g mayonnaise
½ teaspoon freshly ground black pepper, plus more as needed	2 tablespoons capers, rinsed and finely chopped
⅛ teaspoon cayenne pepper	1 tablespoon fresh tarragon
340 g skinless trout fillets, cut	1 teaspoon fresh lemon juice, plus lemon wedges, for serving

1. Preheat the air fryer to 204ºC. 2. In a large bowl, whisk together the cornmeal, flour, baking powder, salt, black pepper, and cayenne. Dip the trout strips in the egg, then toss them in the cornmeal mixture until fully coated. Transfer the trout to a rack set over a baking sheet and liberally spray all over with cooking spray. 3. Transfer half the fish to the air fryer and air fry until the fish is cooked through and golden brown, about 6 minutes. Transfer the fish sticks to a plate and repeat with the remaining fish. 4. Meanwhile, in a bowl, whisk together the mayonnaise, capers, tarragon, and lemon juice. Season the tartar sauce with salt and black pepper. 5. Serve the trout fingers hot along with the tartar sauce and lemon wedges.

Prawns with Swiss Chard

Prep time: 10 minutes | Cook time: 10 minutes |
Serves 4

455 g prawns, peeled and deveined	2 tablespoons apple cider vinegar
½ teaspoon smoked paprika	1 tablespoon coconut oil
70 g Swiss chard, chopped	60 ml heavy cream

1. Mix prawns with smoked paprika and apple cider vinegar. 2. Put the prawns in the air fryer and add coconut oil. 3. Cook the prawns at 176ºC for 10 minutes. 4. Then mix cooked prawns with remaining ingredients and carefully mix.

Asian Marinated Salmon

Prep time: 30 minutes | Cook time: 6 minutes |
Serves 2

Marinade:	1¼ inches thick)
60 ml wheat-free tamari or coconut aminos	Sliced spring onions, for garnish
2 tablespoons lime or lemon juice	Sauce (Optional):
2 tablespoons sesame oil	60 ml beef stock
2 tablespoons powdered sweetener	60 ml wheat-free tamari
2 teaspoons grated fresh ginger	3 tablespoons powdered sweetener
2 cloves garlic, minced	1 tablespoon tomato sauce
½ teaspoon ground black pepper	⅛ teaspoon guar gum or xanthan gum (optional, for thickening)
2 (110 g) salmon fillets (about	

1. Make the marinade: In a medium-sized shallow dish, stir together all the ingredients for the marinade until well combined. Place the salmon in the marinade. Cover and refrigerate for at least 2 hours or overnight. 2. Preheat the air fryer to 204ºC. 3. Remove the salmon fillets from the marinade and place them in the air fryer, leaving space between them. Air fry for 6 minutes, or until the salmon is cooked through and flakes easily with a fork. 4. While the salmon cooks, make the sauce, if using: Place all the sauce ingredients except the guar gum in a medium-sized bowl and stir until well combined. Taste and adjust the sweetness to your liking. While whisking slowly, add the guar gum. Allow the sauce to thicken for 3 to 5 minutes. (The sauce can be made up to 3 days ahead and stored in an airtight container in the fridge.) Drizzle the sauce over the salmon before serving. 5. Garnish the salmon with sliced spring onions before serving. Store leftovers in an airtight container in the fridge for up to 3 days. Reheat in a preheated 176ºC air fryer for 3 minutes, or until heated through.

Browned Prawns Patties

Prep time: 15 minutes | Cook time: 10 to 12 minutes | Serves 4

230 g raw prawns, peeled, deveined and chopped finely
500 g cooked sushi rice
35 g chopped red bell pepper
35 g chopped celery
35 g chopped spring onion
2 teaspoons Worcestershire

sauce
½ teaspoon salt
½ teaspoon garlic powder
½ teaspoon Old Bay seasoning
75 g plain bread crumbs
Cooking spray

1. Preheat the air fryer to 200°C. 2. Put all the ingredients except the bread crumbs and oil in a large bowl and stir to incorporate. 3. Scoop out the prawn mixture and shape into 8 equal-sized patties with your hands, no more than ½-inch thick. Roll the patties in the bread crumbs on a plate and spray both sides with cooking spray. 4. Place the patties in the air fryer basket. You may need to work in batches to avoid overcrowding. 5. Air fry for 10 to 12 minutes, flipping the patties halfway through, or until the outside is crispy brown. 6. Divide the patties among four plates and serve warm.

Jalea

Prep time: 20 minutes | Cook time: 10 minutes | Serves 4

Salsa Criolla☐
½ red onion, thinly sliced
2 tomatoes, diced
1 serrano or jalapeño pepper, deseeded and diced
1 clove garlic, minced
5 g chopped fresh coriander
Pinch of kosher or coarse sea salt
3 limes
Fried Seafood☐
455 g firm, white-fleshed fish such as cod (add an extra 230 g fish if not using prawns)

20 large or jumbo prawns, peeled and deveined
30 g plain flour
40 g cornflour
1 teaspoon garlic powder
1 teaspoon kosher or coarse sea salt
¼ teaspoon cayenne pepper
240 g panko bread crumbs
2 eggs, beaten with 2 tablespoons water
Vegetable oil, for spraying
Mayonnaise or tartar sauce, for serving (optional)

1. To make the Salsa Criolla, combine the red onion, tomatoes, pepper, garlic, cilantro, and salt in a medium bowl. Add the juice and zest of 2 of the limes. Refrigerate the salad while you make the fish. 2. To make the seafood, cut the fish fillets into strips approximately 2 inches long and 1 inch wide. Place the flour, cornstarch, garlic powder, salt, and cayenne pepper on a plate and whisk to combine. Place the panko on a separate plate. Dredge the fish strips in the seasoned flour mixture, shaking off any excess. Dip the strips in the egg mixture, coating them completely, then dredge in the panko, shaking off any excess. Place the fish strips on

a plate or rack. Repeat with the prawns, if using. 3. Spray the air fryer basket with oil, and preheat the air fryer to 204°C. Working in 2 or 3 batches, arrange the fish and prawns in a single layer in the basket, taking care not to crowd the basket. Spray with oil. Air fry for 5 minutes, then flip and air fry for another 4 to 5 minutes until the outside is brown and crisp and the inside of the fish is opaque and flakes easily with a fork. Repeat with the remaining seafood. 4. Place the fried seafood on a platter. Use a slotted spoon to remove the salsa criolla from the bowl, leaving behind any liquid that has accumulated. Place the salsa criolla on top of the fried seafood. Serve immediately with the remaining lime, cut into wedges, and mayonnaise or tartar sauce as desired.

Tuna Melt

Prep time: 3 minutes | Cook time: 10 minutes | Serves 1

Olive or vegetable oil, for spraying
140 g can tuna, drained
1 tablespoon mayonnaise
¼ teaspoon garlic granules, plus

more for garnish
2 teaspoons unsalted butte
2 slices sandwich bread of choice
2 slices Cheddar cheese

1. Line the air fryer basket with baking paper and spray lightly with oil. 2. In a medium bowl, mix together the tuna, mayonnaise, and garlic. 3. Spread 1 teaspoon of butter on each slice of bread and place one slice butter-side down in the prepared basket. 4. Top with a slice of cheese, the tuna mixture, another slice of cheese, and the other slice of bread, butter-side up. 5. Air fry at 204°C for 5 minutes, flip, and cook for another 5 minutes, until browned and crispy. 6. Sprinkle with additional garlic, before cutting in half and serving.

Lemon Pepper Prawns

Prep time: 15 minutes | Cook time: 8 minutes | Serves 2

Olive or vegetable oil, for spraying
340 g medium raw prawns, peeled and deveined
3 tablespoons lemon juice

1 tablespoon olive oil
1 teaspoon lemon pepper
¼ teaspoon paprika
¼ teaspoon granulated garlic

1. Preheat the air fryer to 204°C. Line the air fryer basket with baking paper and spray lightly with oil. 2. In a medium bowl, toss together the prawns, lemon juice, olive oil, lemon pepper, paprika, and garlic until evenly coated. 3. Place the prawns in the prepared basket. 4. Cook for 6 to 8 minutes, or until pink and firm. Serve immediately.

Prawns Curry

Prep time: 30 minutes | Cook time: 10 minutes |
Serves 4

180 ml unsweetened full-fat coconut milk	1 teaspoon ground turmeric
10 g finely chopped yellow onion	1 teaspoon salt
	¼ to ½ teaspoon cayenne pepper
2 teaspoons garam masala	455 g raw prawns (21 to 25 count), peeled and deveined
1 tablespoon minced fresh ginger	
1 tablespoon minced garlic	2 teaspoons chopped fresh coriander

1. In a large bowl, stir together the coconut milk, onion, garam masala, ginger, garlic, turmeric, salt and cayenne, until well blended. 2. Add the prawns and toss until coated with sauce on all sides. Marinate at room temperature for 30 minutes. 3. Transfer the prawns and marinade to a baking pan. Place the pan in the air fryer basket. Set the air fryer to 192°C for 10 minutes, stirring halfway through the cooking time. 4. Transfer the prawns to a serving bowl or platter. Sprinkle with the cilantro and serve.

Nutty Prawns with Amaretto Glaze

Prep time: 30 minutes | Cook time: 10 minutes per batch | Serves 10 to 12

120 g plain flour	oil
½ teaspoon baking powder	185 g sliced almonds
1 teaspoon salt	900 g large prawns (about 32 to 40 prawns), peeled and deveined, tails left on
2 eggs, beaten	
120 ml milk	
2 tablespoons olive or vegetable	470 ml amaretto liqueur

1. Combine the flour, baking powder and salt in a large bowl. Add the eggs, milk and oil and stir until it forms a smooth batter. Coarsely crush the sliced almonds into a second shallow dish with your hands. 2. Dry the prawns well with paper towels. Dip the prawns into the batter and shake off any excess batter, leaving just enough to lightly coat the prawns. Transfer the prawns to the dish with the almonds and coat completely. Place the coated prawns on a plate or baking sheet and when all the prawns have been coated, freeze the prawns for an 1 hour, or as long as a week before air frying. 3. Preheat the air fryer to 204°C. 4. Transfer 8 frozen prawns at a time to the air fryer basket. Air fry for 6 minutes. Turn the prawns over and air fry for an additional 4 minutes. Repeat with the remaining prawns. 5. While the prawns are cooking, bring the Amaretto to a boil in a small saucepan on the stovetop. Lower the heat and simmer until it has reduced and thickened into a glaze, about 10 minutes. 6. Remove the prawns from the air fryer and brush both sides with the warm amaretto glaze. Serve warm.

Crab Cakes with Sriracha Mayonnaise

Prep time: 15 minutes | Cook time: 10 minutes |
Serves 4

Sriracha Mayonnaise☐	40 g diced celery
230 g mayonnaise	455 g lump crab meat
1 tablespoon Sriracha	1 teaspoon Old Bay seasoning
1½ teaspoons freshly squeezed lemon juice	1 egg
Crab Cakes☐	1½ teaspoons freshly squeezed lemon juice
1 teaspoon extra-virgin olive oil	200 g panko bread crumbs, divided
40 g finely diced red bell pepper	
40 g diced onion	Vegetable oil, for spraying

1. Mix the mayonnaise, Sriracha, and lemon juice in a small bowl. Place ⅔ of the mixture in a separate bowl to form the base of the crab cakes. Cover the remaining Sriracha mayonnaise and refrigerate. (This will become dipping sauce for the crab cakes once they are cooked.) 2. Heat the olive oil in a heavy-bottomed, medium skillet over medium-high heat. Add the bell pepper, onion, and celery and sauté for 3 minutes. Transfer the vegetables to the bowl with the reserved ⅔ of Sriracha mayonnaise. Mix in the crab, Old Bay seasoning, egg, and lemon juice. Add 120 g of the panko. Form the crab mixture into 8 cakes. Dredge the cakes in the remaining panko, turning to coat. Place on a baking sheet. Cover and refrigerate for at least 1 hour and up to 8 hours. 3. Preheat the air fryer to 192°C. Spray the air fryer basket with oil. Working in batches as needed so as not to overcrowd the basket, place the chilled crab cakes in a single layer in the basket. Spray the crab cakes with oil. Bake until golden brown, 8 to 10 minutes, carefully turning halfway through cooking. Remove to a platter and keep warm. Repeat with the remaining crab cakes as needed. Serve the crab cakes immediately with Sriracha mayonnaise dipping sauce.

Mediterranean-Style Cod

Prep time: 5 minutes | Cook time: 12 minutes |
Serves 4

4 cod fillets, 170 g each	6 cherry tomatoes, halved
3 tablespoons fresh lemon juice	45 g pitted and sliced kalamata olives
1 tablespoon olive oil	
¼ teaspoon salt	

1. Place cod into an ungreased round nonstick baking dish. Pour lemon juice into dish and drizzle cod with olive oil. Sprinkle with salt. Place tomatoes and olives around baking dish in between fillets. 2. Place dish into air fryer basket. Adjust the temperature to 176°C and bake for 12 minutes, carefully turning cod halfway through cooking. Fillets will be lightly browned, easily flake, and have an internal temperature of at least 64°C when done. Serve warm.

Firecracker Prawns

Prep time: 10 minutes | Cook time: 7 minutes |
Serves 4

455 g medium prawns, peeled and deveined	2 tablespoons Sriracha
2 tablespoons salted butter, melted	¼ teaspoon powdered sweetener
½ teaspoon Old Bay seasoning	60 ml full-fat mayonnaise
¼ teaspoon garlic powder	⅛ teaspoon ground black pepper

1. In a large bowl, toss prawns in butter, Old Bay seasoning, and garlic powder. Place prawns into the air fryer basket. 2. Adjust the temperature to 204°C and set the timer for 7 minutes. 3. Flip the prawns halfway through the cooking time. Prawns will be bright pink when fully cooked. 4. In another large bowl, mix Sriracha, sweetener, mayonnaise, and pepper. Toss prawns in the spicy mixture and serve immediately.

Prawn Caesar Salad

Prep time: 30 minutes | Cook time: 4 to 6 minutes |
Serves 4

340 g fresh large prawns, peeled and deveined	¼ teaspoon freshly ground black pepper, plus additional to season the marinade
1 tablespoon plus 1 teaspoon freshly squeezed lemon juice, divided	735 g mayonnaise
4 tablespoons olive oil or avocado oil, divided	2 tablespoons freshly grated Parmesan cheese
2 garlic cloves, minced, divided	1 teaspoon Dijon mustard
¼ teaspoon sea salt, plus additional to season the marinade	1 tinned anchovy, mashed
	340 g romaine lettuce hearts, torn

1. Place the prawns in a large bowl. Add 1 tablespoon of lemon juice, 1 tablespoon of olive oil, and 1 minced garlic clove. Season with salt and pepper. Toss well and refrigerate for 15 minutes. 2. While the prawns marinates, make the dressing: In a blender, combine the mayonnaise, Parmesan cheese, Dijon mustard, the remaining 1 teaspoon of lemon juice, the anchovy, the remaining minced garlic clove, ¼ teaspoon of salt, and ¼ teaspoon of pepper. Process until smooth. With the blender running, slowly stream in the remaining 3 tablespoons of oil. Transfer the mixture to a jar; seal and refrigerate until ready to serve. 3. Remove the prawns from its marinade and place it in the air fryer basket in a single layer. Set the air fryer to 204°C and air fry for 2 minutes. Flip the prawns and cook for 2 to 4 minutes more, until the flesh turns opaque. 4. Place the romaine in a large bowl and toss with the desired amount of dressing. Top with the prawns and serve immediately.

Scallops Gratiné with Parmesan

Prep time: 10 minutes | Cook time: 9 minutes |
Serves 2

Scallops:	½ teaspoon black pepper
120 ml single cream	455 g sea scallops
45 g grated Parmesan cheese	Topping:
235 g thinly sliced spring onions	30 g panko bread crumbs
5 g chopped fresh parsley	20 g grated Parmesan cheese
3 cloves garlic, minced	Vegetable oil spray
½ teaspoon kosher or coarse sea salt	For Serving:
	Lemon wedges
	Crusty French bread (optional)

1. For the scallops: In a baking pan, combine the single cream, cheese, spring onions, parsley, garlic, salt, and pepper. Stir in the scallops. 2. For the topping: In a small bowl, combine the bread crumbs and cheese. Sprinkle evenly over the scallops. Spray the topping with vegetable oil spray. 3. Place the pan in the air fryer basket. Set the air fryer to 164°C for 6 minutes. Set the air fryer to 204°C for 3 minutes until the topping has browned. 4. To serve: Squeeze the lemon wedges over the gratin and serve with crusty French bread, if desired.

Crispy Prawns with Coriander

Prep time: 40 minutes | Cook time: 10 minutes |
Serves 4

455 g raw large prawns, peeled and deveined with tails on or off	1 egg
	75 g bread crumbs
30 g chopped fresh coriander	Salt and freshly ground black pepper, to taste
Juice of 1 lime	Cooking oil spray
70 g plain flour	240 ml seafood sauce

1. Place the prawns in a resealable plastic bag and add the cilantro and lime juice. Seal the bag. Shake it to combine. Marinate the prawns in the refrigerator for 30 minutes. 2. Place the flour in a small bowl. 3. In another small bowl, beat the egg. 4. Place the bread crumbs in a third small bowl, season with salt and pepper, and stir to combine. 5. Insert the crisper plate into the basket and the basket into the unit. Preheat the unit to 204°C. 6. Remove the prawns from the plastic bag. Dip each in the flour, the egg, and the bread crumbs to coat. Gently press the crumbs onto the prawns. 7. Once the unit is preheated, spray the crisper plate and the basket with cooking oil. Place the prawns in the basket. It is okay to stack them. Spray the prawns with the cooking oil. 8. Cook for 4 minutes, remove the basket and flip the prawns one at a time. Reinsert the basket to resume cooking. 10. When the cooking is complete, the prawns should be crisp. Let cool for 5 minutes. Serve with cocktail sauce.

White Fish with Cauliflower

Prep time: 30 minutes | Cook time: 13 minutes |
Serves 4

230 g cauliflower florets
½ teaspoon English mustard
2 tablespoons butter, room
temperature
½ tablespoon cilantro, minced

2 tablespoons sour cream
340 g cooked white fish
Salt and freshly cracked black
pepper, to taste

1. Boil the cauliflower until tender. Then, purée the cauliflower in your blender. Transfer to a mixing dish. 2. Now, stir in the fish, cilantro, salt, and black pepper. 3. Add the sour cream, English mustard, and butter; mix until everything's well incorporated. Using your hands, shape into patties. 4. Place in the refrigerator for about 2 hours. Cook for 13 minutes at 202°C. Serve with some extra English mustard.

Scallops and Spinach with Cream Sauce

Prep time: 5 minutes | Cook time: 10 minutes |
Serves 2

Vegetable oil spray
280 g frozen spinach, thawed
and drained
8 jumbo sea scallops
Kosher or coarse sea salt, and
black pepper, to taste

180 ml heavy cream
1 tablespoon tomato paste
1 tablespoon chopped fresh
basil
1 teaspoon minced garlic

1. Spray a baking pan with vegetable oil spray. Spread the thawed spinach in an even layer in the bottom of the pan. 2. Spray both sides of the scallops with vegetable oil spray. Season lightly with salt and pepper. Arrange the scallops on top of the spinach. 3. In a small bowl, whisk together the cream, tomato paste, basil, garlic, ½ teaspoon salt, and ½ teaspoon pepper. Pour the sauce over the scallops and spinach. 4. Place the pan in the air fryer basket. Set the air fryer to 176°C for 10 minutes. Use a meat thermometer to ensure the scallops have an internal temperature of 56°C.

Cod with Jalapeño

Prep time: 5 minutes | Cook time: 14 minutes | Serves 4

4 cod fillets, boneless
1 jalapeño, minced

1 tablespoon avocado oil
½ teaspoon minced garlic

1. In the shallow bowl, mix minced jalapeño, avocado oil, and minced garlic. 2. Put the cod fillets in the air fryer basket in one layer and top with minced jalapeño mixture. 3. Cook the fish at 185°C for 7 minutes per side.

Steamed Cod with Garlic and Swiss Chard

Prep time: 5 minutes | Cook time: 12 minutes |
Serves 4

1 teaspoon salt
½ teaspoon dried oregano
½ teaspoon dried thyme
½ teaspoon garlic powder
4 cod fillets

½ white onion, thinly sliced
135 g Swiss chard, washed,
stemmed, and torn into pieces
60 ml olive oil
1 lemon, quartered

1. Preheat the air fryer to 192°C. 2. In a small bowl, whisk together the salt, oregano, thyme, and garlic powder. 3. Tear off four pieces of aluminum foil, with each sheet being large enough to envelop one cod fillet and a quarter of the vegetables. 4. Place a cod fillet in the middle of each sheet of foil, then sprinkle on all sides with the spice mixture. 5. In each foil packet, place a quarter of the onion slices and 30 g Swiss chard, then drizzle 1 tablespoon olive oil and squeeze ¼ lemon over the contents of each foil packet. 6. Fold and seal the sides of the foil packets and then place them into the air fryer basket. Steam for 12 minutes. 7. Remove from the basket, and carefully open each packet to avoid a steam burn.

Lemon-Tarragon Fish en Papillote

Prep time: 10 minutes | Cook time: 15 minutes |
Serves 2

2 tablespoons salted butter,
melted
1 tablespoon fresh lemon juice
½ teaspoon dried tarragon,
crushed, or 2 sprigs fresh
tarragon
1 teaspoon kosher or coarse sea
salt
85 g julienned carrots

435 g julienned fennel, or 1
stalk julienned celery
75 g thinly sliced red bell
pepper
2 cod fillets, 170 g each, thawed
if frozen
Vegetable oil spray
½ teaspoon black pepper

1. In a medium bowl, combine the butter, lemon juice, tarragon, and ½ teaspoon of the salt. Whisk well until you get a creamy sauce. Add the carrots, fennel, and bell pepper and toss to combine; set aside. 2. Cut two squares of baking paper each large enough to hold one fillet and half the vegetables. Spray the fillets with vegetable oil spray. Season both sides with the remaining ½ teaspoon salt and the black pepper. 3. Lay one fillet down on each baking paper square. Top each with half the vegetables. Pour any remaining sauce over the vegetables. 4. Fold over the baking paper and crimp the sides in small, tight folds to hold the fish, vegetables, and sauce securely inside the packet. Place the packets in the air fryer basket. Set the air fryer to 176°C for 15 minutes. 5. Transfer each packet to a plate. Cut open with scissors just before serving (be careful, as the steam inside will be hot).

Butter-Wine Baked Salmon

Prep time: 5 minutes | Cook time: 10 minutes |
Serves 4

4 tablespoons butter, melted	1 tablespoon lime juice
2 cloves garlic, minced	1 teaspoon smoked paprika
Sea salt and ground black pepper, to taste	½ teaspoon onion powder
	4 salmon steaks
60 ml dry white wine or apple cider vinegar	Cooking spray

1. Place all the ingredients except the salmon and oil in a shallow dish and stir to mix well. 2. Add the salmon steaks, turning to coat well on both sides. Transfer the salmon to the refrigerator to marinate for 30 minutes. 3. Preheat the air fryer to 182°C. 4. Place the salmon steaks in the air fryer basket, discarding any excess marinade. Spray the salmon steaks with cooking spray. 5. Air fry for about 10 minutes, flipping the salmon steaks halfway through, or until cooked to your preferred doneness. 6. Divide the salmon steaks among four plates and serve.

Sole and Asparagus Bundles

Prep time: 10 minutes | Cook time: 14 minutes |
Serves 2

230 g asparagus, trimmed	softened
1 teaspoon extra-virgin olive oil, divided	1 small shallot, minced
Salt and pepper, to taste	1 tablespoon chopped fresh tarragon
4 (85 g) skinless sole fillets, ⅛ to ¼ inch thick	¼ teaspoon lemon zest plus ½ teaspoon juice
4 tablespoons unsalted butter,	Vegetable oil spray

1. Preheat the air fryer to 150°C. 2. Toss asparagus with ½ teaspoon oil, pinch salt, and pinch pepper in a bowl. Cover and microwave until bright green and just tender, about 3 minutes, tossing halfway through microwaving. Uncover and set aside to cool slightly. 3. Make foil sling for air fryer basket by folding 1 long sheet of aluminum foil so it is 4 inches wide. Lay sheet of foil widthwise across basket, pressing foil into and up sides of basket. Fold excess foil as needed so that edges of foil are flush with top of basket. Lightly spray foil and basket with vegetable oil spray. 4. Pat sole dry with paper towels and season with salt and pepper. Arrange fillets skinned side up on cutting board, with thicker ends closest to you. Arrange asparagus evenly across base of each fillet, then tightly roll fillets away from you around asparagus to form tidy bundles. 5. Rub bundles evenly with remaining ½ teaspoon oil and arrange seam side down on sling in prepared basket. Bake until asparagus is tender and sole flakes apart when gently prodded with a paring knife, 14 to 18 minutes, using a sling to rotate bundles halfway through cooking. 6. Combine butter, shallot, tarragon, and lemon zest and juice in a bowl. Using sling, carefully remove sole bundles from air fryer and transfer to individual plates. Top evenly with butter mixture and serve.

Salmon Spring Rolls

Prep time: 20 minutes | Cook time: 8 to 10 minutes |
Serves 4

230 g salmon fillet	sliced
1 teaspoon toasted sesame oil	1 carrot, shredded
1 onion, sliced	10 g chopped fresh flat-leaf
8 rice paper wrappers	parsley
1 yellow bell pepper, thinly	15 g chopped fresh basil

1. Put the salmon in the air fryer basket and drizzle with the sesame oil. Add the onion. Air fry at 188°C for 8 to 10 minutes, or until the salmon just flakes when tested with a fork and the onion is tender. 2. Meanwhile, fill a small shallow bowl with warm water. One at a time, dip the rice paper wrappers into the water and place on a work surface. 3. Top each wrapper with one-eighth each of the salmon and onion mixture, yellow bell pepper, carrot, parsley, and basil. Roll up the wrapper, folding in the sides, to enclose the ingredients. 4. If you like, bake in the air fryer at 192°C for 7 to 9 minutes, until the rolls are crunchy. Cut the rolls in half to serve.

Italian Tuna Roast

Prep time: 15 minutes | Cook time: 21 to 24 minutes
| Serves 8

Cooking spray	oil
1 tablespoon Italian seasoning	1 teaspoon lemon juice
⅛ teaspoon ground black pepper	1 (900 g) tuna loin, 3 to 4 inches thick
1 tablespoon extra-light olive	

1. Spray baking dish with cooking spray and place in air fryer basket. Preheat the air fryer to 200°C. 2. Mix together the Italian seasoning, pepper, oil, and lemon juice. 3. Using a dull table knife or butter knife, pierce top of tuna about every half inch: Insert knife into top of tuna roast and pierce almost all the way to the bottom. 4. Spoon oil mixture into each of the holes and use the knife to push seasonings into the tuna as deeply as possible. 5. Spread any remaining oil mixture on all outer surfaces of tuna. 6. Place tuna roast in baking dish and roast for 20 minutes. Check temperature with a meat thermometer. Cook for an additional 1 to 4 minutes or until temperature reaches 64°C. 7. Remove basket from the air fryer and let tuna sit in the basket for 10 minutes.

Salmon Fritters with Courgette

Prep time: 15 minutes | Cook time: 12 minutes | Serves 4

2 tablespoons almond flour	1 teaspoon avocado oil
1 courgette, grated	½ teaspoon ground black
1 egg, beaten	pepper
170 g salmon fillet, diced	

1. Mix almond flour with courgette, egg, salmon, and ground black pepper. 2. Then make the fritters from the salmon mixture. 3. Sprinkle the air fryer basket with avocado oil and put the fritters inside. 4. Cook the fritters at 192ºC for 6 minutes per side.

Prawns with Smoky Tomato Dressing

Prep time: 5 minutes | Cook time: 8 minutes | Serves 2

3 tablespoons mayonnaise	salt
1 tablespoon ketchup	455 g large raw prawns (21 to
1 tablespoon minced garlic	25 count), peeled (tails left on)
1 teaspoon Sriracha	and deveined
½ teaspoon smoked paprika	Vegetable oil spray
½ teaspoon kosher or coarse sea	50 g chopped spring onions

1. In a large bowl, combine the mayonnaise, ketchup, garlic, Sriracha, paprika, and salt. Add the prawns and toss to coat with the sauce. 2. Spray the air fryer basket with vegetable oil spray. Place the prawns in the basket. Set the air fryer to 176ºC for 8 minutes, tossing and spraying the prawns with vegetable oil spray halfway through the cooking time. 3. Sprinkle with the chopped spring onions before serving.

Mouthwatering Cod over Creamy Leek Noodles

Prep time: 10 minutes | Cook time: 24 minutes | Serves 4

1 small leek, sliced into long thin noodles	Coating:
120 ml heavy cream	20 g grated Parmesan cheese
2 cloves garlic, minced	2 tablespoons mayonnaise
1 teaspoon fine sea salt, divided	2 tablespoons unsalted butter,
4 cod fillets, 110 g each (about	softened
1 inch thick)	1 tablespoon chopped fresh
½ teaspoon ground black	thyme, or ½ teaspoon dried
pepper	thyme leaves, plus more for
	garnish

1. Preheat the air fryer to 176ºC. 2. Place the leek noodles in a casserole dish or a pan that will fit in your air fryer. 3. In a small bowl, stir together the cream, garlic, and ½ teaspoon of the salt.

Pour the mixture over the leeks and cook in the air fryer for 10 minutes, or until the leeks are very tender. 4. Pat the fish dry and season with the remaining ½ teaspoon of salt and the pepper. When the leeks are ready, open the air fryer and place the fish fillets on top of the leeks. Air fry for 8 to 10 minutes, until the fish flakes easily with a fork (the thicker the fillets, the longer this will take). 5. While the fish cooks, make the coating: In a small bowl, combine the Parmesan, mayo, butter, and thyme. 6. When the fish is ready, remove it from the air fryer and increase the heat to 218ºC (or as high as your air fryer can go). Spread the fillets with a ½-inch-thick to ¾-inch-thick layer of the coating. 7. Place the fish back in the air fryer and air fry for 3 to 4 minutes, until the coating browns. 8. Garnish with fresh or dried thyme, if desired. Store leftovers in an airtight container in the refrigerator for up to 3 days. Reheat in a casserole dish in a preheated 176ºC air fryer for 6 minutes, or until heated through.

Friday Night Fish-Fry

Prep time: 10 minutes | Cook time: 10 minutes | Serves 4

1 large egg	pepper
45 g powdered Parmesan cheese	4 cod fillets, 110 g each
1 teaspoon smoked paprika	Chopped fresh oregano or
¼ teaspoon celery salt	parsley, for garnish (optional)
¼ teaspoon ground black	Lemon slices, for serving (optional)

1. Spray the air fryer basket with avocado oil. Preheat the air fryer to 204ºC. 2. Crack the egg in a shallow bowl and beat it lightly with a fork. Combine the Parmesan cheese, paprika, celery salt, and pepper in a separate shallow bowl. 3. One at a time, dip the fillets into the egg, then dredge them in the Parmesan mixture. Using your hands, press the Parmesan onto the fillets to form a nice crust. As you finish, place the fish in the air fryer basket. 4. Air fry the fish in the air fryer for 10 minutes, or until it is cooked through and flakes easily with a fork. Garnish with fresh oregano or parsley and serve with lemon slices, if desired. 5. Store leftovers in an airtight container in the refrigerator for up to 3 days. Reheat in a preheated 204ºC air fryer for 5 minutes, or until warmed through.

chilli Tilapia

Prep time: 5 minutes | Cook time: 20 minutes | Serves 4

4 tilapia fillets, boneless	1 tablespoon avocado oil
1 teaspoon chilli flakes	1 teaspoon mustard
1 teaspoon dried oregano	

1. Rub the tilapia fillets with chilli flakes, dried oregano, avocado oil, and mustard and put in the air fryer. 2. Cook it for 10 minutes per side at 182ºC.

Pesto Prawns with Wild Rice Pilaf

Prep time: 5 minutes | Cook time: 5 minutes | Serves 4

455 g medium prawns, peeled and deveined
60 g pesto sauce

1 lemon, sliced
390 g cooked wild rice pilaf

1. Preheat the air fryer to 182ºC. 2. In a medium bowl, toss the prawns with the pesto sauce until well coated. 3. Place the prawns in a single layer in the air fryer basket. Put the lemon slices over the prawns and roast for 5 minutes. 4. Remove the lemons and discard. Serve a quarter of the prawns over 100 g wild rice with some favorite steamed vegetables.

chilli Prawns

Prep time: 10 minutes | Cook time: 8 minutes | Serves 2

8 prawns, peeled and deveined
Salt and black pepper, to taste
½ teaspoon ground cayenne pepper
½ teaspoon garlic powder

½ teaspoon ground cumin
½ teaspoon red chilli flakes
Cooking spray

1. Preheat the air fryer to 172ºC. Spritz the air fryer basket with cooking spray. 2. Toss the remaining ingredients in a large bowl until the prawns are well coated. 3. Spread the coated prawns evenly in the basket and spray them with cooking spray. 4. Air fry for 8 minutes, flipping the prawns halfway through, or until the prawns are pink. 5. Remove the prawns from the basket to a plate.

Chapter 5 Poultry

Bacon-Wrapped Stuffed Chicken Breasts

Prep time: 15 minutes | Cook time: 30 minutes | Serves 4

80 g chopped frozen spinach, thawed and squeezed dry	2 large boneless, skinless chicken breasts, butterflied and pounded to ½-inch thickness
55 g cream cheese, softened	
20 g grated Parmesan cheese	4 teaspoons salt-free Cajun seasoning
1 jalapeño, seeded and chopped	
½ teaspoon kosher salt	6 slices bacon
1 teaspoon black pepper	

1. In a small bowl, combine the spinach, cream cheese, Parmesan cheese, jalapeño, salt, and pepper. Stir until well combined. 2. Place the butterflied chicken breasts on a flat surface. Spread the cream cheese mixture evenly across each piece of chicken. Starting with the narrow end, roll up each chicken breast, ensuring the filling stays inside. Season chicken with the Cajun seasoning, patting it in to ensure it sticks to the meat. 3. Wrap each breast in 3 slices of bacon. Place in the air fryer basket. Set the air fryer to 180°C for 30 minutes. Use a meat thermometer to ensure the chicken has reached an internal temperature of 76°C. 4. Let the chicken stand 5 minutes before slicing each rolled-up breast in half to serve.

Crispy Duck with Cherry Sauce

Prep time: 10 minutes | Cook time: 33 minutes | Serves 2 to 4

1 whole duck (2.3 kg), split in half, back and rib bones removed	1 shallot, minced
	120 ml sherry
	240 g cherry preserves
1 teaspoon olive oil	240 ml chicken stock
Salt and freshly ground black pepper, to taste	1 teaspoon white wine vinegar
	1 teaspoon fresh thyme leaves
Cherry Sauce:	Salt and freshly ground black pepper, to taste
1 tablespoon butter	

1. Preheat the air fryer to 200°C. 2. Trim some of the fat from the duck. Rub olive oil on the duck and season with salt and pepper. Place the duck halves in the air fryer basket, breast side up and facing the centre of the basket. 3. Air fry the duck for 20 minutes. Turn the duck over and air fry for another 6 minutes. 4. While duck is air frying, make the cherry sauce. Melt the butter in a large sauté pan. Add the shallot and sauté until it is just starting to brown, about 2 to 3 minutes. Add the sherry and deglaze the pan by scraping up any brown bits from the bottom of the pan. Simmer the liquid for a few minutes, until it has reduced by half. Add the cherry preserves, chicken stock and white wine vinegar. Whisk well to combine all the ingredients. Simmer the sauce until it thickens and coats the back of a spoon, about 5 to 7 minutes. Season with salt and pepper and stir in the fresh thyme leaves. 5. When the air fryer timer goes off, spoon some cherry sauce over the duck and continue to air fry at 200°C for 4 more minutes. Then, turn the duck halves back over so that the breast side is facing up. Spoon more cherry sauce over the top of the duck, covering the skin completely. Air fry for 3 more minutes and then remove the duck to a plate to rest for a few minutes. 6. Serve the duck in halves, or cut each piece in half again for a smaller serving. Spoon any additional sauce over the duck or serve it on the side.

Chicken Jalfrezi

Prep time: 15 minutes | Cook time: 15 minutes | Serves 4

Chicken:	1 teaspoon kosher salt
450 g boneless, skinless chicken thighs, cut into 2 or 3 pieces each	½ to 1 teaspoon cayenne pepper
	Sauce:
1 medium onion, chopped	55 g tomato sauce
1 large green bell pepper, stemmed, seeded, and chopped	1 tablespoon water
	1 teaspoon garam masala
2 tablespoons olive oil	½ teaspoon kosher salt
1 teaspoon ground turmeric	½ teaspoon cayenne pepper
1 teaspoon garam masala	Side salad, rice, or naan bread, for serving

1. For the chicken: In a large bowl, combine the chicken, onion, bell pepper, oil, turmeric, garam masala, salt, and cayenne. Stir and toss until well combined. 2. Place the chicken and vegetables in the air fryer basket. Set the air fryer to 180°C for 15 minutes, stirring and tossing halfway through the cooking time. Use a meat thermometer to ensure the chicken has reached an internal temperature of 76°C. 3. Meanwhile, for the sauce: In a small microwave-safe bowl, combine the tomato sauce, water, garam masala, salt, and cayenne. Microwave on high for 1 minute. Remove and stir. Microwave for another minute; set aside. 4. When the chicken is cooked, remove and place chicken and vegetables in a large bowl. Pour the sauce over all. Stir and toss to coat the chicken and vegetables evenly. 5. Serve with rice, naan, or a side salad.

Chicken Paillard

Prep time: 10 minutes | Cook time: 10 minutes | Serves 2

2 large eggs, room temperature
1 tablespoon water
40 g powdered Parmesan cheese or pork dust
2 teaspoons dried thyme leaves
1 teaspoon ground black pepper
2 (140 g) boneless, skinless chicken breasts, pounded to ½ inch thick

Lemon Butter Sauce:
2 tablespoons unsalted butter, melted
2 teaspoons lemon juice
¼ teaspoon finely chopped fresh thyme leaves, plus more for garnish
⅛ teaspoon fine sea salt
Lemon slices, for serving

1. Spray the air fryer basket with avocado oil. Preheat the air fryer to 200ºC. 2. Beat the eggs in a shallow dish, then add the water and stir well. 3. In a separate shallow dish, mix together the Parmesan, thyme, and pepper until well combined. 4. One at a time, dip the chicken breasts in the eggs and let any excess drip off, then dredge both sides of the chicken in the Parmesan mixture. As you finish, set the coated chicken in the air fryer basket. 5. Roast the chicken in the air fryer for 5 minutes, then flip the chicken and cook for another 5 minutes, or until cooked through and the internal temperature reaches 76ºC. 6. While the chicken cooks, make the lemon butter sauce: In a small bowl, mix together all the sauce ingredients until well combined. 7. Plate the chicken and pour the sauce over it. Garnish with chopped fresh thyme and serve with lemon slices. 8. Store leftovers in an airtight container in the refrigerator for up to 4 days. Reheat in a preheated 200ºC air fryer for 5 minutes, or until heated through.

Spice-Rubbed Turkey Breast

Prep time: 5 minutes | Cook time: 45 to 55 minutes | Serves 10

1 tablespoon sea salt
1 teaspoon paprika
1 teaspoon onion powder
1 teaspoon garlic powder
½ teaspoon freshly ground

black pepper
1.8 kg bone-in, skin-on turkey breast
2 tablespoons unsalted butter, melted

1. In a small bowl, combine the salt, paprika, onion powder, garlic powder, and pepper. 2. Sprinkle the seasonings all over the turkey. Brush the turkey with some of the melted butter. 3. Set the air fryer to 180ºC. . Place the turkey in the air fryer basket, skin-side down, and roast for 25 minutes. 4. Flip the turkey and brush it with the remaining butter. Continue cooking for another 20 to 30 minutes, until an instant-read thermometer reads 70ºC. 5. Remove the turkey breast from the air fryer. Tent a piece of aluminum foil over the turkey, and allow it to rest for about 5 minutes before serving.

Italian Crispy Chicken

Prep time: 10 minutes | Cook time: 20 minutes | Serves 4

2 (115 g) boneless, skinless chicken breasts
2 egg whites, beaten
120 g Italian bread crumbs
45 g grated Parmesan cheese
2 teaspoons Italian seasoning

Salt and freshly ground black pepper, to taste
Cooking oil spray
180 g marinara sauce
110 g shredded Mozzarella cheese

1. With your knife blade parallel to the cutting board, cut the chicken breasts in half horizontally to create 4 thin cutlets. On a solid surface, pound the cutlets to flatten them. You can use your hands, a rolling pin, a kitchen mallet, or a meat hammer. 2. Pour the egg whites into a bowl large enough to dip the chicken. 3. In another bowl large enough to dip a chicken cutlet in, stir together the bread crumbs, Parmesan cheese, and Italian seasoning, and season with salt and pepper. 4. Dip each cutlet into the egg whites and into the breadcrumb mixture to coat. 5. Insert the crisper plate into the basket and the basket into the unit. Preheat the unit by selecting AIR FRY, setting the temperature to 190ºC, and setting the time to 3 minutes. Select START/STOP to begin. 6. Once the unit is preheated, spray the crisper plate with cooking oil. Working in batches, place 2 chicken cutlets into the basket. Spray the top of the chicken with cooking oil. 7. Select AIR FRY, set the temperature to 190ºC, and set the time to 7 minutes. Select START/STOP to begin. 8. When the cooking is complete, repeat steps 6 and 7 with the remaining cutlets. 9. Top the chicken cutlets with the marinara sauce and shredded Mozzarella cheese. If the chicken will fit into the basket without stacking, you can prepare all 4 at once. Otherwise, do this 2 cutlets at a time. 10. Select AIR FRY, set the temperature to 190ºC, and set the time to 3 minutes. Select START/STOP to begin. 11. The cooking is complete when the cheese is melted and the chicken reaches an internal temperature of 76ºC. Cool for 5 minutes before serving.

Chicken Nuggets

Prep time: 10 minutes | Cook time: 15 minutes | Serves 4

450 g chicken mince thighs
110 g shredded Mozzarella cheese
1 large egg, whisked

½ teaspoon salt
¼ teaspoon dried oregano
¼ teaspoon garlic powder

1. In a large bowl, combine all ingredients. Form mixture into twenty nugget shapes, about 2 tablespoons each. 2. Place nuggets into ungreased air fryer basket, working in batches if needed. Adjust the temperature to (190ºC and air fry for 15 minutes, turning nuggets halfway through cooking. Let cool 5 minutes before serving.

Blackened Cajun Chicken Tenders

Prep time: 10 minutes | Cook time: 17 minutes | Serves 4

2 teaspoons paprika	pepper
1 teaspoon chili powder	2 tablespoons coconut oil
½ teaspoon garlic powder	450 g boneless, skinless chicken
½ teaspoon dried thyme	tenders
¼ teaspoon onion powder	60 ml full-fat ranch dressing
⅛ teaspoon ground cayenne	

1. In a small bowl, combine all seasonings. 2. Drizzle oil over chicken tenders and then generously coat each tender in the spice mixture. Place tenders into the air fryer basket. 3. Adjust the temperature to (190ºC and air fry for 17 minutes. 4. Tenders will be 76ºC internally when fully cooked. Serve with ranch dressing for dipping.

Lemon-Basil Turkey Breasts

Prep time: 30 minutes | Cook time: 58 minutes | Serves 4

2 tablespoons olive oil	1 teaspoon fresh basil leaves,
900 g turkey breasts, bone-in,	chopped
skin-on	2 tablespoons lemon zest,
Coarse sea salt and ground	grated
black pepper, to taste	

1. Rub olive oil on all sides of the turkey breasts; sprinkle with salt, pepper, basil, and lemon zest. 2. Place the turkey breasts skin side up on the parchment-lined air fryer basket. 3. Cook in the preheated air fryer at 170ºC for 30 minutes. Now, turn them over and cook an additional 28 minutes. 4. Serve with lemon wedges, if desired. Bon appétit!

Classic Chicken Kebab

Prep time: 35 minutes | Cook time: 25 minutes | Serves 4

60 ml olive oil	450 g boneless skinless chicken
1 teaspoon garlic powder	thighs, cut into 1-inch pieces
1 teaspoon onion powder	1 red bell pepper, cut into 1-inch
1 teaspoon ground cumin	pieces
½ teaspoon dried oregano	1 red onion, cut into 1-inch
½ teaspoon dried basil	pieces
60 ml lemon juice	1 courgette, cut into 1-inch
1 tablespoon apple cider	pieces
vinegar	12 cherry tomatoes
Olive oil cooking spray	

1. In a large bowl, mix together the olive oil, garlic powder, onion powder, cumin, oregano, basil, lemon juice, and apple cider vinegar. 2. Spray six skewers with olive oil cooking spray. 3. On each skewer, slide on a piece of chicken, then a piece of bell pepper, onion, courgette, and finally a tomato and then repeat. Each skewer should have at least two pieces of each item. 4. Once all of the skewers are prepared, place them in a 9-by-13-inch baking dish and pour the olive oil marinade over the top of the skewers. Turn each skewer so that all sides of the chicken and vegetables are coated. 5. Cover the dish with plastic wrap and place it in the refrigerator for 30 minutes. 6. After 30 minutes, preheat the air fryer to 192ºC. (If using a grill attachment, make sure it is inside the air fryer during preheating.) 7. Remove the skewers from the marinade and lay them in a single layer in the air fryer basket. If the air fryer has a grill attachment, you can also lay them on this instead. 8. Cook for 10 minutes. Rotate the kebabs, then cook them for 15 minutes more. 9. Remove the skewers from the air fryer and let them rest for 5 minutes before serving.

Teriyaki Chicken Thighs with Lemony Snow Peas

Prep time: 30 minutes | Cook time: 34 minutes | Serves 4

60 ml chicken broth	1 tablespoon sugar
½ teaspoon grated fresh ginger	170 g mangetout, strings
⅛ teaspoon red pepper flakes	removed
1½ tablespoons soy sauce	⅛ teaspoon lemon zest
4 (140 g) bone-in chicken	1 garlic clove, minced
thighs, trimmed	¼ teaspoon salt
1 tablespoon mirin	Ground black pepper, to taste
½ teaspoon cornflour	½ teaspoon lemon juice

1. Combine the broth, ginger, pepper flakes, and soy sauce in a large bowl. Stir to mix well. 2. Pierce 10 to 15 holes into the chicken skin. Put the chicken in the broth mixture and toss to coat well. Let sit for 10 minutes to marinate. 3. Preheat the air fryer to 206ºC. 4. Transfer the marinated chicken on a plate and pat dry with paper towels. 5. Scoop 2 tablespoons of marinade in a microwave-safe bowl and combine with mirin, cornflour and sugar. Stir to mix well. Microwave for 1 minute or until frothy and has a thick consistency. Set aside. 6. Arrange the chicken in the preheated air fryer, skin side up, and air fry for 25 minutes or until the internal temperature of the chicken reaches at least 76ºC. Gently turn the chicken over halfway through. 7. When the frying is complete, brush the chicken skin with marinade mixture. Air fryer the chicken for 5 more minutes or until glazed. 8. Remove the chicken from the air fryer and reserve ½ teaspoon of chicken fat remains in the air fryer. Allow the chicken to cool for 10 minutes. 9. Meanwhile, combine the reserved chicken fat, snow peas, lemon zest, garlic, salt, and ground black pepper in a small bowl. Toss to coat well. 10. Transfer the snow peas in the air fryer and air fry for 3 minutes or until soft. Remove the peas from the air fryer and toss with lemon juice. 11. Serve the chicken with lemony snow peas.

Herbed Turkey Breast with Simple Dijon Sauce

Prep time: 5 minutes | Cook time: 30 minutes | Serves 4

1 teaspoon chopped fresh sage	1½ teaspoons sea salt
1 teaspoon chopped fresh tarragon	1 teaspoon ground black pepper
1 teaspoon chopped fresh thyme leaves	1 (900 g) turkey breast
	3 tablespoons Dijon mustard
1 teaspoon chopped fresh rosemary leaves	3 tablespoons butter, melted
	Cooking spray

1. Preheat the air fryer to 200ºC. Spritz the air fryer basket with cooking spray. 2. Combine the herbs, salt, and black pepper in a small bowl. Stir to mix well. Set aside. 3. Combine the Dijon mustard and butter in a separate bowl. Stir to mix well. 4. Rub the turkey with the herb mixture on a clean work surface, then brush the turkey with Dijon mixture. 5. Arrange the turkey in the preheated air fryer basket. Air fry for 30 minutes or until an instant-read thermometer inserted in the thickest part of the turkey breast reaches at least 76ºC. 6. Transfer the cooked turkey breast on a large plate and slice to serve.

One-Dish Chicken and Rice

Prep time: 10 minutes | Cook time: 40 minutes | Serves 4

190 g long-grain white rice, rinsed and drained	3 cloves garlic, minced
	1 tablespoon toasted sesame oil
120 g cut frozen green beans (do not thaw)	1 teaspoon kosher salt
	1 teaspoon black pepper
1 tablespoon minced fresh ginger	450 g chicken wings, preferably drumettes

1. In a baking pan, combine the rice, green beans, ginger, garlic, sesame oil, salt, and pepper. Stir to combine. Place the chicken wings on top of the rice mixture. 2. Cover the pan with foil. Make a long slash in the foil to allow the pan to vent steam. Place the pan in the air fryer basket. Set the air fryer to (190ºC for 30 minutes. 3. Remove the foil. Set the air fryer to 200ºC for 10 minutes, or until the wings have browned and rendered fat into the rice and vegetables, turning the wings halfway through the cooking time.

Buffalo Chicken Cheese Sticks

Prep time: 5 minutes | Cook time: 8 minutes | Serves 2

140 g shredded cooked chicken	cheese
60 ml buffalo sauce	1 large egg
220 g shredded Mozzarella	55 g crumbled feta

1. In a large bowl, mix all ingredients except the feta. Cut a piece of parchment to fit your air fryer basket and press the mixture into a ½-inch-thick circle. 2. Sprinkle the mixture with feta and place into the air fryer basket. 3. Adjust the temperature to 200ºC and air fry for 8 minutes. 4. After 5 minutes, flip over the cheese mixture. 5. Allow to cool 5 minutes before cutting into sticks. Serve warm.

Fajita-Stuffed Chicken Breast

Prep time: 15 minutes | Cook time: 25 minutes | Serves 4

2 (170 g) boneless, skinless chicken breasts	seeded and sliced
	1 tablespoon coconut oil
¼ medium white onion, peeled and sliced	2 teaspoons chili powder
	1 teaspoon ground cumin
1 medium green bell pepper,	½ teaspoon garlic powder

1. Slice each chicken breast completely in half lengthwise into two even pieces. Using a meat tenderizer, pound out the chicken until it's about ¼-inch thickness. 2. Lay each slice of chicken out and place three slices of onion and four slices of green pepper on the end closest to you. Begin rolling the peppers and onions tightly into the chicken. Secure the roll with either toothpicks or a couple pieces of butcher's twine. 3. Drizzle coconut oil over chicken. Sprinkle each side with chili powder, cumin, and garlic powder. Place each roll into the air fryer basket. 4. Adjust the temperature to 180ºC and air fry for 25 minutes. 5. Serve warm.

Golden Tenders

Prep time: 10 minutes | Cook time: 15 minutes | Serves 4

120 g panko bread crumbs	black pepper
1 tablespoon paprika	16 chicken tenders
½ teaspoon salt	115 g mayonnaise
¼ teaspoon freshly ground	Olive oil spray

1. In a medium bowl, stir together the panko, paprika, salt, and pepper. 2. In a large bowl, toss together the chicken tenders and mayonnaise to coat. Transfer the coated chicken pieces to the bowl of seasoned panko and dredge to coat thoroughly. Press the coating onto the chicken with your fingers. 3. Insert the crisper plate into the basket and the basket into the unit. Preheat the unit by selecting AIR FRY, setting the temperature to 180ºC, and setting the time to 3 minutes. Select START/STOP to begin. 4. Once the unit is preheated, place a parchment paper liner into the basket. Place the chicken into the basket and spray it with olive oil. 5. Select AIR FRY, set the temperature to 180ºC, and set the time to 15 minutes. Select START/STOP to begin. 6. When the cooking is complete, the tenders will be golden brown and a food thermometer inserted into the chicken should register 76ºC. For more even browning, remove the basket halfway through cooking and flip the tenders. Give them an extra spray of olive oil and reinsert the basket to resume cooking. This ensures they are crispy and brown all over. 7. When the cooking is complete, serve.

Ranch Chicken Wings

Prep time: 10 minutes | Cook time: 40 minutes | Serves 4

2 tablespoons water	1 (30 g) envelope ranch salad
2 tablespoons hot pepper sauce	dressing mix
2 tablespoons unsalted butter,	1 teaspoon paprika
melted	4 1.8 kg chicken wings, tips
2 tablespoons apple cider	removed
vinegar	Cooking oil spray

1. In a large bowl, whisk the water, hot pepper sauce, melted butter, vinegar, salad dressing mix, and paprika until combined. 2. Add the wings and toss to coat. At this point, you can cover the bowl and marinate the wings in the refrigerator for 4 to 24 hours for best results. However, you can just let the wings stand for 30 minutes in the refrigerator. 3. Insert the crisper plate into the basket and the basket into the unit. Preheat the unit by selecting AIR FRY, setting the temperature to 200ºC, and setting the time to 3 minutes. Select START/STOP to begin. 4. Once the unit is preheated, spray the crisper plate with cooking oil. Working in batches, put half the wings into the basket; it is okay to stack them. Refrigerate the remaining wings. 5. Select AIR FRY, set the temperature to 200ºC, and set the time to 20 minutes. Select START/STOP to begin. 6. After 5 minutes, remove the basket and shake it. Reinsert the basket to resume cooking. Remove and shake the basket every 5 minutes, three more times, until the chicken is browned and glazed and a food thermometer inserted into the wings registers 76ºC. 7. Repeat steps 4, 5, and 6 with the remaining wings. 8. When the cooking is complete, serve warm.

Spinach and Feta Stuffed Chicken Breasts

Prep time: 10 minutes | Cook time: 27 minutes | Serves 4

1 (280 g) package frozen	black pepper
spinach, thawed and drained	4 boneless chicken breasts
well	Salt and freshly ground black
80 g feta cheese, crumbled	pepper, to taste
½ teaspoon freshly ground	1 tablespoon olive oil

1. Prepare the filling. Squeeze out as much liquid as possible from the thawed spinach. Rough chop the spinach and transfer it to a mixing bowl with the feta cheese and the freshly ground black pepper. 2. Prepare the chicken breast. Place the chicken breast on a cutting board and press down on the chicken breast with one hand to keep it stabilized. Make an incision about 1-inch long in the fattest side of the breast. Move the knife up and down inside the chicken breast, without poking through either the top or the bottom, or the other side of the breast. The inside pocket should be about 3-inches long, but the opening should only be about 1-inch wide. If this is too difficult, you can make the incision longer, but you will have to be more careful when cooking the chicken breast since this will expose more of the stuffing. 3. Once you have prepared the chicken breasts, use your fingers to stuff the filling into each pocket, spreading the mixture down as far as you can. 4. Preheat the air fryer to 190ºC. 5. Lightly brush or spray the air fryer basket and the chicken breasts with olive oil. Transfer two of the stuffed chicken breasts to the air fryer. Air fry for 12 minutes, turning the chicken breasts over halfway through the cooking time. Remove the chicken to a resting plate and air fry the second two breasts for 12 minutes. Return the first batch of chicken to the air fryer with the second batch and air fry for 3 more minutes. When the chicken is cooked, an instant read thermometer should register 76ºC in the thickest part of the chicken, as well as in the stuffing. 6. Remove the chicken breasts and let them rest on a cutting board for 2 to 3 minutes. Slice the chicken on the bias and serve with the slices fanned out.

Pomegranate-Glazed Chicken with Couscous Salad

Prep time: 25 minutes | Cook time: 20 minutes | Serves 4

3 tablespoons plus 2 teaspoons	80 g couscous
pomegranate molasses	1 tablespoon minced fresh
½ teaspoon ground cinnamon	parsley
1 teaspoon minced fresh thyme	60 g cherry tomatoes, quartered
Salt and ground black pepper,	1 scallion, white part minced,
to taste	green part sliced thin on bias
2 (340 g) bone-in split chicken	1 tablespoon extra-virgin olive
breasts, trimmed	oil
60 ml chicken broth	30 g feta cheese, crumbled
60 ml water	Cooking spray

1. Preheat the air fryer to 180ºC. Spritz the air fryer basket with cooking spray. 2. Combine 3 tablespoons of pomegranate molasses, cinnamon, thyme, and ⅛ teaspoon of salt in a small bowl. Stir to mix well. Set aside. 3. Place the chicken breasts in the preheated air fryer, skin side down, and spritz with cooking spray. Sprinkle with salt and ground black pepper. 4. Air fry the chicken for 10 minutes, then brush the chicken with half of pomegranate molasses mixture and flip. Air fry for 5 more minutes. 5. Brush the chicken with remaining pomegranate molasses mixture and flip. Air fry for another 5 minutes or until the internal temperature of the chicken breasts reaches at least 76ºC. 6. Meanwhile, pour the broth and water in a pot and bring to a boil over medium-high heat. Add the couscous and sprinkle with salt. Cover and simmer for 7 minutes or until the liquid is almost absorbed. 7. Combine the remaining ingredients, except for the cheese, with cooked couscous in a large bowl. Toss to mix well. Scatter with the feta cheese. 8. When the air frying is complete, remove the chicken from the air fryer and allow to cool for 10 minutes. Serve with vegetable and couscous salad.

Italian Chicken with Sauce

Prep time: 15 minutes | Cook time: 20 minutes | Serves 4

2 large skinless chicken breasts (about 565 g)	1 egg, lightly beaten
Salt and freshly ground black pepper	1 tablespoon olive oil
50 g almond meal	225 g no-sugar-added marinara sauce
45 g grated Parmesan cheese	4 slices Mozzarella cheese or
2 teaspoons Italian seasoning	110 g shredded Mozzarella

1. Preheat the air fryer to 180°C. 2. Slice the chicken breasts in half horizontally to create 4 thinner chicken breasts. Working with one piece at a time, place the chicken between two pieces of parchment paper and pound with a meat mallet or rolling pin to flatten to an even thickness. Season both sides with salt and freshly ground black pepper. 3. In a large shallow bowl, combine the almond meal, Parmesan, and Italian seasoning; stir until thoroughly combined. Place the egg in another large shallow bowl. 4. Dip the chicken in the egg, followed by the almond meal mixture, pressing the mixture firmly into the chicken to create an even coating. 5. Working in batches if necessary, arrange the chicken breasts in a single layer in the air fryer basket and coat both sides lightly with olive oil. Pausing halfway through the cooking time to flip the chicken, air fry for 15 minutes, or until a thermometer inserted into the thickest part registers 76°C. 6. Spoon the marinara sauce over each piece of chicken and top with the Mozzarella cheese. Air fry for an additional 3 to 5 minutes until the cheese is melted.

Easy Chicken Fingers

Prep time: 20 minutes | Cook time: 30 minutes | Makes 12 chicken fingers

60 g all-purpose flour	breasts, each cut into 4 strips
240 g panko breadcrumbs	Kosher salt and freshly ground
2 tablespoons rapeseed oil	black pepper, to taste
1 large egg	Cooking spray
3 boneless and skinless chicken	

1. Preheat the air fryer to 180°C. Spritz the air fryer basket with cooking spray. 2. Pour the flour in a large bowl. Combine the panko and rapeseed oil on a shallow dish. Whisk the egg in a separate bowl. 3. Rub the chicken strips with salt and ground black pepper on a clean work surface, then dip the chicken in the bowl of flour. Shake the excess off and dunk the chicken strips in the bowl of whisked egg, then roll the strips over the panko to coat well. 4. Arrange 4 strips in the air fryer basket each time and air fry for 10 minutes or until crunchy and lightly browned. Flip the strips halfway through. Repeat with remaining ingredients. 5. Serve immediately.

Spice-Rubbed Chicken Thighs

Prep time: 10 minutes | Cook time: 25 minutes | Serves 4

4 (115 g) bone-in, skin-on chicken thighs	2 teaspoons chili powder
½ teaspoon salt	1 teaspoon paprika
½ teaspoon garlic powder	1 teaspoon ground cumin
	1 small lime, halved

1. Pat chicken thighs dry and sprinkle with salt, garlic powder, chili powder, paprika, and cumin. 2. Squeeze juice from ½ lime over thighs. Place thighs into ungreased air fryer basket. Adjust the temperature to 190°C and roast for 25 minutes, turning thighs halfway through cooking. Thighs will be crispy and browned with an internal temperature of at least 76°C when done. 3. Transfer thighs to a large serving plate and drizzle with remaining lime juice. Serve warm.

Chicken Strips with Satay Sauce

Prep time: 15 minutes | Cook time: 10 minutes | Serves 4

4 (170 g) boneless, skinless chicken breasts, sliced into 16 (1-inch) strips	fresh ginger
	½ teaspoon hot sauce
1 teaspoon fine sea salt	⅛ teaspoon stevia glycerite, or
1 teaspoon paprika	2 to 3 drops liquid stevia
Sauce:	For Garnish/Serving (Optional):
60 g creamy almond butter (or sunflower seed butter for nut-free)	15 g chopped coriander leaves
	Red pepper flakes
2 tablespoons chicken broth	Sea salt flakes
1½ tablespoons coconut vinegar or unseasoned rice vinegar	Thinly sliced red, orange, and yellow bell peppers
1 clove garlic, minced	Special Equipment:
1 teaspoon peeled and minced	16 wooden or bamboo skewers, soaked in water for 15 minutes

1. Spray the air fryer basket with avocado oil. Preheat the air fryer to 200°C. 2. Thread the chicken strips onto the skewers. Season on all sides with the salt and paprika. Place the chicken skewers in the air fryer basket and air fry for 5 minutes, flip, and cook for another 5 minutes, until the chicken is cooked through and the internal temperature reaches 76°C. 3. While the chicken skewers cook, make the sauce: In a medium-sized bowl, stir together all the sauce ingredients until well combined. Taste and adjust the sweetness and heat to your liking. 4. Garnish the chicken with coriander, red pepper flakes, and salt flakes, if desired, and serve with sliced bell peppers, if desired. Serve the sauce on the side. 5. Store leftovers in an airtight container in the fridge for up to 4 days or in the freezer for up to a month. Reheat in a preheated 180°C air fryer for 3 minutes per side, or until heated through.

Butter and Bacon Chicken

Prep time: 10 minutes | Cook time: 65 minutes | Serves 6

1 (1.8 kg) whole chicken
2 tablespoons salted butter, softened
1 teaspoon dried thyme
½ teaspoon garlic powder

1 teaspoon salt
½ teaspoon ground black pepper
6 slices sugar-free bacon

1. Pat chicken dry with a paper towel, then rub with butter on all sides. Sprinkle thyme, garlic powder, salt, and pepper over chicken. 2. Place chicken into ungreased air fryer basket, breast side up. Lay strips of bacon over chicken and secure with toothpicks. 3. Adjust the temperature to 180ºC and air fry for 65 minutes. Halfway through cooking, remove and set aside bacon and flip chicken over. Chicken will be done when the skin is golden and crispy and the internal temperature is at least 76ºC. Serve warm with bacon.

Italian Chicken Thighs

Prep time: 5 minutes | Cook time: 20 minutes | Serves 2

4 bone-in, skin-on chicken thighs
2 tablespoons unsalted butter, melted
1 teaspoon dried parsley

1 teaspoon dried basil
½ teaspoon garlic powder
¼ teaspoon onion powder
¼ teaspoon dried oregano

1. Brush chicken thighs with butter and sprinkle remaining ingredients over thighs. Place thighs into the air fryer basket. 2. Adjust the temperature to 190ºC and roast for 20 minutes. 3. Halfway through the cooking time, flip the thighs. 4. When fully cooked, internal temperature will be at least 76ºC and skin will be crispy. Serve warm.

Smoky Chicken Leg Quarters

Prep time: 30 minutes | Cook time: 23 to 27 minutes | Serves 6

120 ml avocado oil
2 teaspoons smoked paprika
1 teaspoon sea salt
1 teaspoon garlic powder
½ teaspoon dried rosemary

½ teaspoon dried thyme
½ teaspoon freshly ground black pepper
900 g bone-in, skin-on chicken leg quarters

1. In a blender or small bowl, combine the avocado oil, smoked paprika, salt, garlic powder, rosemary, thyme, and black pepper. 2. Place the chicken in a shallow dish or large zip-top bag. Pour the marinade over the chicken, making sure all the legs are coated. Cover and marinate for at least 2 hours or overnight. 3. Place the chicken in a single layer in the air fryer basket, working in batches if necessary. Set the air fryer to 200ºC and air fry for 15 minutes. Flip the chicken legs, then reduce the temperature to 180ºC. . Cook for 8 to 12 minutes more, until an instant-read thermometer reads 70ºC when inserted into the thickest piece of chicken. 4. Allow to rest for 5 to 10 minutes before serving.

Chicken Patties

Prep time: 15 minutes | Cook time: 12 minutes | Serves 4

450 g chicken thigh mince
110 g shredded Mozzarella cheese
1 teaspoon dried parsley

½ teaspoon garlic powder
¼ teaspoon onion powder
1 large egg
60 g pork rinds, finely ground

1. In a large bowl, mix chicken mince, Mozzarella, parsley, garlic powder, and onion powder. Form into four patties. 2. Place patties in the freezer for 15 to 20 minutes until they begin to firm up. 3. Whisk egg in a medium bowl. Place the ground pork rinds into a large bowl. 4. Dip each chicken patty into the egg and then press into pork rinds to fully coat. Place patties into the air fryer basket. 5. Adjust the temperature to 180ºC and air fry for 12 minutes. 6. Patties will be firm and cooked to an internal temperature of 76ºC when done. Serve immediately.

Hawaiian Chicken Bites

Prep time: 1 hour 15 minutes | Cook time: 15 minutes | Serves 4

120 ml pineapple juice
2 tablespoons apple cider vinegar
½ tablespoon minced ginger
120 g ketchup
2 garlic cloves, minced

110 g brown sugar
2 tablespoons sherry
120 ml soy sauce
4 chicken breasts, cubed
Cooking spray

1. Combine the pineapple juice, cider vinegar, ginger, ketchup, garlic, and sugar in a saucepan. Stir to mix well. Heat over low heat for 5 minutes or until thickened. Fold in the sherry and soy sauce. 2. Dunk the chicken cubes in the mixture. Press to submerge. Wrap the bowl in plastic and refrigerate to marinate for at least an hour. 3. Preheat the air fryer to 180ºC. Spritz the air fryer basket with cooking spray. 4. Remove the chicken cubes from the marinade. Shake the excess off and put in the preheated air fryer. Spritz with cooking spray. 5. Air fry for 15 minutes or until the chicken cubes are glazed and well browned. Shake the basket at least three times during the frying. 6. Serve immediately.

Tex-Mex Chicken Breasts

Prep time: 10 minutes | Cook time: 17 to 20 minutes | Serves 4

450 g low-sodium boneless, skinless chicken breasts, cut into 1-inch cubes
1 medium onion, chopped
1 red bell pepper, chopped
1 jalapeño pepper, minced

2 teaspoons olive oil
115 g canned low-sodium black beans, rinsed and drained
130 g low-sodium salsa
2 teaspoons chili powder

1. Preheat the air fryer to 200ºC. 2. In a medium metal bowl, mix the chicken, onion, bell pepper, jalapeño, and olive oil. Roast for 10 minutes, stirring once during cooking. 3. Add the black beans, salsa, and chili powder. Roast for 7 to 10 minutes more, stirring once, until the chicken reaches an internal temperature of 76ºC on a meat thermometer. Serve immediately.

Juicy Paprika Chicken Breast

Prep time: 5 minutes | Cook time: 30 minutes | Serves 4

Oil, for spraying
4 (170 g) boneless, skinless chicken breasts
1 tablespoon olive oil
1 tablespoon paprika

1 tablespoon packed light brown sugar
½ teaspoon cayenne pepper
½ teaspoon onion powder
½ teaspoon granulated garlic

1. Line the air fryer basket with parchment and spray lightly with oil. 2. Brush the chicken with the olive oil. 3. In a small bowl, mix together the paprika, brown sugar, cayenne pepper, onion powder, and garlic and sprinkle it over the chicken. 4. Place the chicken in the prepared basket. You may need to work in batches, depending on the size of your air fryer. 5. Air fry at 180ºC for 15 minutes, flip, and cook for another 15 minutes, or until the internal temperature reaches 76ºC. Serve immediately.

Crispy Dill Chicken Strips

Prep time: 30 minutes | Cook time: 10 minutes | Serves 4

2 whole boneless, skinless chicken breasts (about 450 g each), halved lengthwise
230 ml Italian dressing
110 g finely crushed crisps

1 tablespoon dried dill weed
1 tablespoon garlic powder
1 large egg, beaten
1 to 2 tablespoons oil

1. In a large resealable bag, combine the chicken and Italian dressing. Seal the bag and refrigerate to marinate at least 1 hour. 2. In a shallow dish, stir together the potato chips, dill, and garlic powder. Place the beaten egg in a second shallow dish. 3. Remove the chicken from the marinade. Roll the chicken pieces in the egg and the crisp mixture, coating thoroughly. 4. Preheat the air fryer to 170ºC. Line the air fryer basket with parchment paper. 5. Place the coated chicken on the parchment and spritz with oil. 6. Cook for 5 minutes. Flip the chicken, spritz it with oil, and cook for 5 minutes more until the outsides are crispy and the insides are no longer pink.

Jerk Chicken Thighs

Prep time: 30 minutes | Cook time: 15 to 20 minutes | Serves 6

2 teaspoons ground coriander
1 teaspoon ground allspice
1 teaspoon cayenne pepper
1 teaspoon ground ginger
1 teaspoon salt
1 teaspoon dried thyme

½ teaspoon ground cinnamon
½ teaspoon ground nutmeg
900 g boneless chicken thighs, skin on
2 tablespoons olive oil

1. In a small bowl, combine the coriander, allspice, cayenne, ginger, salt, thyme, cinnamon, and nutmeg. Stir until thoroughly combined. 2. Place the chicken in a baking dish and use paper towels to pat dry. Thoroughly coat both sides of the chicken with the spice mixture. Cover and refrigerate for at least 2 hours, preferably overnight. 3. Preheat the air fryer to 180ºC. 4. Working in batches if necessary, arrange the chicken in a single layer in the air fryer basket and lightly coat with the olive oil. Pausing halfway through the cooking time to flip the chicken, air fry for 15 to 20 minutes, until a thermometer inserted into the thickest part registers 76ºC.

Cheese-Encrusted Chicken Tenderloins with Peanuts

Prep time: 10 minutes | Cook time: 25 minutes | Serves 4

45 g grated Parmesan cheese
½ teaspoon garlic powder
1 teaspoon red pepper flakes
Sea salt and ground black pepper, to taste

2 tablespoons peanut oil
680 g chicken tenderloins
2 tablespoons peanuts, roasted and roughly chopped
Cooking spray

1. Preheat the air fryer to 180ºC. Spritz the air fryer basket with cooking spray. 2. Combine the Parmesan cheese, garlic powder, red pepper flakes, salt, black pepper, and peanut oil in a large bowl. Stir to mix well. 3. Dip the chicken tenderloins in the cheese mixture, then press to coat well. Shake the excess off. 4. Transfer the chicken tenderloins in the air fryer basket. Air fry for 12 minutes or until well browned. Flip the tenderloin halfway through. You may need to work in batches to avoid overcrowding. 5. Transfer the chicken tenderloins on a large plate and top with roasted peanuts before serving.

Chicken Parmesan

Prep time: 15 minutes | Cook time: 10 minutes | Serves 4

Oil, for spraying
2 (230 g) boneless, skinless chicken breasts
120 g Italian-style bread crumbs
20 g grated Parmesan cheese,
plus 45 g shredded
4 tablespoons unsalted butter, melted
115 g marinara sauce

1. Preheat the air fryer to 180ºC. Line the air fryer basket with parchment and spray lightly with oil. 2. Cut each chicken breast in half through its thickness to make 4 thin cutlets. Using a meat tenderizer, pound each cutlet until it is about ¾ inch thick. 3. On a plate, mix together the bread crumbs and grated Parmesan cheese. 4. Lightly brush the chicken with the melted butter, then dip into the bread crumb mixture. 5. Place the chicken in the prepared basket and spray lightly with oil. You may need to work in batches, depending on the size of your air fryer. 6. Cook for 6 minutes. Top the chicken with the marinara and shredded Parmesan cheese, dividing evenly. Cook for another 3 to 4 minutes, or until golden brown, crispy, and the internal temperature reaches 76ºC.

Thai Chicken with Cucumber and Chili Salad

Prep time: 25 minutes | Cook time: 25 minutes | Serves 6

2 (570 g) small chickens, giblets discarded
1 tablespoon fish sauce
6 tablespoons chopped fresh coriander
2 teaspoons lime zest
1 teaspoon ground coriander
2 garlic cloves, minced
2 tablespoons packed light brown sugar
2 teaspoons vegetable oil
Salt and ground black pepper,
to taste
1 English cucumber, halved lengthwise and sliced thin
1 Thai chili, stemmed, deseeded, and minced
2 tablespoons chopped dry-roasted peanuts
1 small shallot, sliced thinly
1 tablespoon lime juice
Lime wedges, for serving
Cooking spray

1. Arrange a chicken on a clean work surface, remove the backbone with kitchen shears, then pound the chicken breast to flat. Cut the breast in half. Repeat with the remaining chicken. 2. Loose the breast and thigh skin with your fingers, then pat the chickens dry and pierce about 10 holes into the fat deposits of the chickens. Tuck the wings under the chickens. 3. Combine 2 teaspoons of fish sauce, coriander, lime zest, coriander, garlic, 4 teaspoons of sugar, 1 teaspoon of vegetable oil, ½ teaspoon of salt, and ⅛ teaspoon of ground black pepper in a small bowl. Stir to mix well. 4. Rub the fish sauce mixture under the breast and thigh skin of the game chickens, then let sit for 10 minutes to marinate. 5. Preheat the air fryer to 200ºC. Spritz the air fryer basket with cooking spray. 6. Arrange the marinated chickens in the preheated air fryer, skin side down. 7. Air fry for 15 minutes, then gently turn the game hens

over and air fry for 10 more minutes or until the skin is golden brown and the internal temperature of the chickens reads at least 76ºC. 8. Meanwhile, combine all the remaining ingredients, except for the lime wedges, in a large bowl and sprinkle with salt and black pepper. Toss to mix well. 9. Transfer the fried chickens on a large plate, then sit the salad aside and squeeze the lime wedges over before serving.

Coriander Lime Chicken Thighs

Prep time: 15 minutes | Cook time: 22 minutes | Serves 4

4 bone-in, skin-on chicken thighs
1 teaspoon baking powder
½ teaspoon garlic powder
2 teaspoons chili powder
1 teaspoon cumin
2 medium limes
5 g chopped fresh coriander

1. Pat chicken thighs dry and sprinkle with baking powder. 2. In a small bowl, mix garlic powder, chili powder, and cumin and sprinkle evenly over thighs, gently rubbing on and under chicken skin. 3. Cut one lime in half and squeeze juice over thighs. Place chicken into the air fryer basket. 4. Adjust the temperature to 190ºC and roast for 22 minutes. 5. Cut other lime into four wedges for serving and garnish cooked chicken with wedges and coriander.

Fiesta Chicken Plate

Prep time: 15 minutes | Cook time: 12 to 15 minutes | Serves 4

450 g boneless, skinless chicken breasts (2 large breasts)
2 tablespoons lime juice
1 teaspoon cumin
½ teaspoon salt
40 g grated Pepper Jack cheese
1 (455 g) can refried beans
130 g salsa
30 g shredded lettuce
1 medium tomato, chopped
2 avocados, peeled and sliced
1 small onion, sliced into thin rings
Sour cream
Tortilla chips (optional)

1. Split each chicken breast in half lengthwise. 2. Mix lime juice, cumin, and salt together and brush on all surfaces of chicken breasts. 3. Place in air fryer basket and air fry at 200ºC for 12 to 15 minutes, until well done. 4. Divide the cheese evenly over chicken breasts and cook for an additional minute to melt cheese. 5. While chicken is cooking, heat refried beans on stovetop or in microwave. 6. When ready to serve, divide beans among 4 plates. Place chicken breasts on top of beans and spoon salsa over. Arrange the lettuce, tomatoes, and avocados artfully on each plate and scatter with the onion rings. 7. Pass sour cream at the table and serve with tortilla chips if desired.

Easy Chicken Nachos

Prep time: 5 minutes | Cook time: 5 minutes | Serves 8

Oil, for spraying
420 g shredded cooked chicken
1 (30 g) package ranch seasoning
60 g sour cream

55 g corn tortilla chips
75 g bacon bits
235 g shredded Cheddar cheese
1 tablespoon chopped spring onions

1. Line the air fryer basket with parchment and spray lightly with oil. 2. In a small bowl, mix together the chicken, ranch seasoning, and sour cream. 3. Place the tortilla chips in the prepared basket and top with the chicken mixture. Add the bacon bits, Cheddar cheese, and spring onions. 4. Air fry at 220°C for 3 to 5 minutes, or until heated through and the cheese is melted.

African Merguez Meatballs

Prep time: 30 minutes | Cook time: 10 minutes | Serves 4

450 g chicken mince
2 garlic cloves, finely minced
1 tablespoon sweet Hungarian paprika
1 teaspoon kosher salt
1 teaspoon sugar
1 teaspoon ground cumin

½ teaspoon black pepper
½ teaspoon ground fennel
½ teaspoon ground coriander
½ teaspoon cayenne pepper
¼ teaspoon ground allspice

1. In a large bowl, gently mix the chicken, garlic, paprika, salt, sugar, cumin, black pepper, fennel, coriander, cayenne, and allspice until all the ingredients are incorporated. Let stand for 30 minutes at room temperature, or cover and refrigerate for up to 24 hours. 2. Form the mixture into 16 meatballs. Arrange them in a single layer in the air fryer basket. Set the air fryer to 200°C for 10 minutes, turning the meatballs halfway through the cooking time. Use a meat thermometer to ensure the meatballs have reached an internal temperature of 76°C.

Italian Flavour Chicken Breasts with Roma Tomatoes

Prep time: 10 minutes | Cook time: 60 minutes | Serves 8

1.4 kg chicken breasts, bone-in
1 teaspoon minced fresh basil
1 teaspoon minced fresh rosemary
2 tablespoons minced fresh parsley
1 teaspoon cayenne pepper

½ teaspoon salt
½ teaspoon freshly ground black pepper
4 medium Roma tomatoes, halved
Cooking spray

1. Preheat the air fryer to 190°C. Spritz the air fryer basket with cooking spray. 2. Combine all the ingredients, except for the chicken breasts and tomatoes, in a large bowl. Stir to mix well. 3. Dunk the chicken breasts in the mixture and press to coat well. 4. Transfer the chicken breasts in the preheated air fryer. You may need to work in batches to avoid overcrowding. 5. Air fry for 25 minutes or until the internal temperature of the thickest part of the breasts reaches at least 76°C. Flip the breasts halfway through the cooking time. 6. Remove the cooked chicken breasts from the basket and adjust the temperature to 180°C. 7. Place the tomatoes in the air fryer and spritz with cooking spray. Sprinkle with a touch of salt and cook for 10 minutes or until tender. Shake the basket halfway through the cooking time. 8. Serve the tomatoes with chicken breasts on a large serving plate.

Chapter 6 Beef, Pork, and Lamb

Bacon-Wrapped Hot Dogs with Mayo-Ketchup Sauce

Prep time: 5 minutes | Cook time: 10 to 12 minutes | Serves 5

10 thin slices of bacon	60 ml mayonnaise
5 pork hot dogs, halved	4 tablespoons ketchup
1 teaspoon cayenne pepper	1 teaspoon rice vinegar
Sauce:	1 teaspoon chili powder

1. Preheat the air fryer to 200°C. 2. Arrange the slices of bacon on a clean work surface. One by one, place the halved hot dog on one end of each slice, season with cayenne pepper and wrap the hot dog with the bacon slices and secure with toothpicks as needed. 3. Work in batches, place half the wrapped hot dogs in the air fryer basket and air fry for 10 to 12 minutes or until the bacon becomes browned and crispy. 4. Make the sauce: Stir all the ingredients for the sauce in a small bowl. Wrap the bowl in plastic and set in the refrigerator until ready to serve. 5. Transfer the hot dogs to a platter and serve hot with the sauce.

Jalapeño Popper Pork Chops

Prep time: 15 minutes | Cook time: 6 to 8 minutes | Serves 4

800 g bone-in, loin pork chops	110 g sliced bacon, cooked and crumbled
Sea salt and freshly ground black pepper, to taste	110 g Cheddar cheese, shredded
170 g cream cheese, at room temperature	1 jalapeño, seeded and diced
	1 teaspoon garlic powder

1. Cut a pocket into each pork chop, lengthwise along the side, making sure not to cut it all the way through. Season the outside of the chops with salt and pepper. 2. In a small bowl, combine the cream cheese, bacon, Cheddar cheese, jalapeño, and garlic powder. Divide this mixture among the pork chops, stuffing it into the pocket of each chop. 3. Set the air fryer to 204°C. Place the pork chops in the air fryer basket in a single layer, working in batches if necessary. Air fry for 3 minutes. Flip the chops and cook for 3 to 5 minutes more, until an instant-read thermometer reads 64°C. 4. Allow the chops to rest for 5 minutes, then serve warm.

Deconstructed Chicago Dogs

Prep time: 10 minutes | Cook time: 7 minutes | Serves 4

4 hot dogs	peppers, diced
2 large dill pickles	For Garnish (Optional):
60 ml diced onions	Wholegrain or Dijon mustard
1 tomato, cut into ½-inch dice	Celery salt
4 pickled or brined jalapeno	Poppy seeds

1. Spray the air fryer basket with avocado oil. Preheat the air fryer to 204°C. 2. Place the hot dogs in the air fryer basket and air fry for 5 to 7 minutes, until hot and slightly crispy. 3. While the hot dogs cook, quarter one of the dill pickles lengthwise, so that you have 4 pickle spears. Finely dice the other pickle. 4. When the hot dogs are done, transfer them to a serving platter and arrange them in a row, alternating with the pickle spears. Top with the diced pickles, onions, tomato, and jalapeno peppers. Drizzle mustard on top and garnish with celery salt and poppy seeds, if desired. 5. Best served fresh. Store leftover hot dogs in an airtight container in the refrigerator for up to 3 days. Reheat in a preheated 200°C air fryer for 2 minutes, or until warmed through.

Rosemary Roast Beef

Prep time: 30 minutes | Cook time: 30 to 35 minutes | Serves 8

1 (900 g) beef roasting joint, tied with kitchen string	2 teaspoons minced garlic
Sea salt and freshly ground black pepper, to taste	2 tablespoons finely chopped fresh rosemary
	60 ml avocado oil

1. Season the roast generously with salt and pepper. 2. In a small bowl, whisk together the garlic, rosemary, and avocado oil. Rub this all over the roast. Cover loosely with aluminum foil or plastic wrap and refrigerate for at least 12 hours or up to 2 days. 3. Remove the roast from the refrigerator and allow to sit at room temperature for about 1 hour. 4. Set the air fryer to 164°C. Place the roast in the air fryer basket and roast for 15 minutes. Flip the roast and cook for 15 to 20 minutes more, until the meat is browned and an instant-read thermometer reads 49°C at the thickest part (for medium-rare). 5. Transfer the meat to a cutting board, and let it rest for 15 minutes before thinly slicing and serving.

Italian Steak Rolls

Prep time: 30 minutes | Cook time: 9 minutes | Serves 4

1 tablespoon vegetable oil	1 (280 g) package frozen
2 cloves garlic, minced	spinach, thawed and squeezed
2 teaspoons dried Italian	dry
seasoning	120 ml diced jarred roasted red
1 teaspoon coarse or flaky salt	pepper
1 teaspoon black pepper	235 ml shredded Mozzarella
450 g bavette or skirt steak, ¼	cheese
to ½ inch thick	

1. In a large bowl, combine the oil, garlic, Italian seasoning, salt, and pepper. Whisk to combine. Add the steak to the bowl, turning to ensure the entire steak is covered with the seasonings. Cover and marinate at room temperature for 30 minutes or in the refrigerator for up to 24 hours. 2. Lay the steak on a flat surface. Spread the spinach evenly over the steak, leaving a ¼-inch border at the edge. Evenly top each steak with the red pepper and cheese. 3. Starting at a long end, roll up the steak as tightly as possible, ending seam side down. Use 2 or 3 wooden toothpicks to hold the roll together. Using a sharp knife, cut the roll in half so that it better fits in the air fryer basket. 4. Place the steak roll, seam side down, in the air fryer basket. Set the air fryer to 204°C for 9 minutes. Use a meat thermometer to ensure the steak has reached an internal temperature of 64°C. (It is critical to not overcook bavette steak, so as to not toughen the meat.) 5. Let the steak rest for 10 minutes before cutting into slices to serve.

Apple Cornbread Stuffed Pork Loin

Prep time: 15 minutes | Cook time: 1 hour | Serves 4 to 6

4 strips of bacon, chopped	2 tablespoons butter
1 Granny Smith apple, peeled,	1 shallot, minced
cored and finely chopped	1 Granny Smith apple, peeled,
2 teaspoons fresh thyme leaves	cored and finely chopped
60 ml chopped fresh parsley	3 sprigs fresh thyme
475 ml cubed cornbread	2 tablespoons flour
120 ml chicken stock	235 ml chicken stock
Salt and freshly ground black	120 ml apple cider
pepper, to taste	Salt and freshly ground black
1 (900 g) boneless pork loin	pepper, to taste
Apple Gravy:	

1. Preheat the air fryer to 204°C. 2. Add the bacon to the air fryer and air fry for 6 to 8 minutes until crispy. While the bacon is cooking, combine the apple, fresh thyme, parsley and cornbread in a bowl and toss well. Moisten the mixture with the chicken stock and season to taste with salt and freshly ground black pepper. Add the cooked bacon to the mixture. 3. Butterfly the pork loin by holding it flat on the cutting board with one hand, while slicing into the pork loin parallel to the cutting board with the other. Slice into the longest side of the pork loin, but stop before you cut all the way through. You should then be able to open the pork loin up like a book, making it twice as wide as it was when you started. Season the inside of the pork with salt and freshly ground black pepper. 4. Spread the cornbread mixture onto the butterflied pork loin, leaving a one-inch border around the edge of the pork. Roll the pork loin up around the stuffing to enclose the stuffing, and tie the rolled pork in several places with kitchen twine or secure with toothpicks. Try to replace any stuffing that falls out of the roast as you roll it, by stuffing it into the ends of the rolled pork. Season the outside of the pork with salt and freshly ground black pepper. 5. Preheat the air fryer to 182°C. 6. Place the stuffed pork loin into the air fryer, seam side down. Air fry the pork loin for 15 minutes at 182°C. Turn the pork loin over and air fry for an additional 15 minutes. Turn the pork loin a quarter turn and air fry for an additional 15 minutes. Turn the pork loin over again to expose the fourth side, and air fry for an additional 10 minutes. The pork loin should register 68°C on an instant read thermometer when it is finished. 7. While the pork is cooking, make the apple gravy. Preheat a saucepan over medium heat on the stovetop and melt the butter. Add the shallot, apple and thyme sprigs and sauté until the apple starts to soften and brown a little. Add the flour and stir for a minute or two. Whisk in the stock and apple cider vigorously to prevent the flour from forming lumps. Bring the mixture to a boil to thicken and season to taste with salt and pepper. 8. Transfer the pork loin to a resting plate and loosely tent with foil, letting the pork rest for at least 5 minutes before slicing and serving with the apple gravy poured over the top.

Minute Steak Roll-Ups

Prep time: 30 minutes | Cook time: 8 to 10 minutes | Serves 4

4 minute steaks (170 g each)	onion
1 (450 g) bottle Italian dressing	120 ml finely chopped green
1 teaspoon salt	pepper
½ teaspoon freshly ground	120 ml finely chopped
black pepper	mushrooms
120 ml finely chopped brown	1 to 2 tablespoons oil

1. In a large resealable bag or airtight storage container, combine the steaks and Italian dressing. Seal the bag and refrigerate to marinate for 2 hours. 2. Remove the steaks from the marinade and place them on a cutting board. Discard the marinade. Evenly season the steaks with salt and pepper. 3. In a small bowl, stir together the onion, pepper, and mushrooms. Sprinkle the onion mixture evenly over the steaks. Roll up the steaks, jelly roll-style, and secure with toothpicks. 4. Preheat the air fryer to 204°C. 5. Place the steaks in the air fryer basket. 6. Cook for 4 minutes. Flip the steaks and spritz them with oil. Cook for 4 to 6 minutes more until the internal temperature reaches 64°C. Let rest for 5 minutes before serving.

Kielbasa and Cabbage

Prep time: 10 minutes | Cook time: 20 to 25 minutes | Serves 4

450 g smoked kielbasa sausage, sliced into ½-inch pieces

1 head cabbage, very coarsely chopped

½ brown onion, chopped

2 cloves garlic, chopped

2 tablespoons olive oil

½ teaspoon salt

½ teaspoon freshly ground black pepper

60 ml water

1. Preheat the air fryer to 204°C. 2. In a large bowl, combine the sausage, cabbage, onion, garlic, olive oil, salt, and black pepper. Toss until thoroughly combined. 3. Transfer the mixture to the basket of the air fryer and pour the water over the top. Pausing two or three times during the cooking time to shake the basket, air fry for 20 to 25 minutes, until the sausage is browned and the vegetables are tender.

Herb-Roasted Beef Tips with Onions

Prep time: 5 minutes | Cook time: 10 minutes | Serves 4

450 g rib eye steak, cubed

2 garlic cloves, minced

2 tablespoons olive oil

1 tablespoon fresh oregano

1 teaspoon salt

½ teaspoon black pepper

1 brown onion, thinly sliced

1. Preheat the air fryer to 192°C. 2. In a medium bowl, combine the steak, garlic, olive oil, oregano, salt, pepper, and onion. Mix until all of the beef and onion are well coated. 3. Put the seasoned steak mixture into the air fryer basket. Roast for 5 minutes. Stir and roast for 5 minutes more. 4. Let rest for 5 minutes before serving with some favorite sides.

Herb-Crusted Lamb Chops

Prep time: 10 minutes | Cook time: 5 minutes | Serves 2

1 large egg

2 cloves garlic, minced

60 ml finely crushed pork scratchings

60 ml pre-grated Parmesan cheese

1 tablespoon chopped fresh oregano leaves

1 tablespoon chopped fresh rosemary leaves

1 teaspoon chopped fresh thyme

leaves

½ teaspoon ground black pepper

4 (1-inch-thick) lamb chops

For Garnish/Serving (Optional):

Sprigs of fresh oregano

Sprigs of fresh rosemary

Sprigs of fresh thyme

Lavender flowers

Lemon slices

1. Spray the air fryer basket with avocado oil. Preheat the air fryer to 204°C. 2. Beat the egg in a shallow bowl, add the garlic, and stir well to combine. In another shallow bowl, mix together the crushed pork scratchings, Parmesan, herbs, and pepper. 3. One at a time, dip the lamb chops into the egg mixture, shake off the excess egg, and then dredge them in the Parmesan mixture. Use your hands to coat the chops well in the Parmesan mixture and form a nice crust on all sides; if necessary, dip the chops again in both the egg and the Parmesan mixture. 4. Place the lamb chops in the air fryer basket, leaving space between them, and air fry for 5 minutes, or until the internal temperature reaches 64°C for medium doneness. Allow to rest for 10 minutes before serving. 5. Garnish with sprigs of oregano, rosemary, and thyme, and lavender flowers, if desired. Serve with lemon slices, if desired. 6. Best served fresh. Store leftovers in an airtight container in the fridge for up to 4 days. Serve chilled over a salad, or reheat in a 176°C air fryer for 3 minutes, or until heated through.

Baby Back Ribs

Prep time: 5 minutes | Cook time: 25 minutes | Serves 4

900 g baby back ribs

2 teaspoons chili powder

1 teaspoon paprika

½ teaspoon onion granules

½ teaspoon garlic powder

¼ teaspoon ground cayenne pepper

120 ml low-carb, sugar-free barbecue sauce

1. Rub ribs with all ingredients except barbecue sauce. Place into the air fryer basket. 2. Adjust the temperature to 204°C and roast for 25 minutes. 3. When done, ribs will be dark and charred with an internal temperature of at least 85°C. Brush ribs with barbecue sauce and serve warm.

Almond and Caraway Crust Steak

Prep time: 16 minutes | Cook time: 10 minutes | Serves 4

80 ml almond flour

2 eggs

2 teaspoons caraway seeds

4 beef steaks

2 teaspoons garlic powder

1 tablespoon melted butter

Fine sea salt and cayenne pepper, to taste

1. Generously coat steaks with garlic powder, caraway seeds, salt, and cayenne pepper. 2. In a mixing dish, thoroughly combine melted butter with seasoned crumbs. In another bowl, beat the eggs until they're well whisked. 3. First, coat steaks with the beaten egg; then, coat beef steaks with the buttered crumb mixture. Place the steaks in the air fryer basket; cook for 10 minutes at 179°C. Bon appétit!

Bone-in Pork Chops

Prep time: 5 minutes | Cook time: 10 to 12 minutes | Serves 2

450 g bone-in pork chops	¼ teaspoon cayenne pepper
1 tablespoon avocado oil	Sea salt and freshly ground
1 teaspoon smoked paprika	black pepper, to taste
½ teaspoon onion granules	

1. Brush the pork chops with the avocado oil. In a small dish, mix together the smoked paprika, onion granules, cayenne pepper, and salt and black pepper to taste. Sprinkle the seasonings over both sides of the pork chops. 2. Set the air fryer to 204°C. Place the chops in the air fryer basket in a single layer, working in batches if necessary. Air fry for 10 to 12 minutes, until an instant-read thermometer reads 64°C at the chops' thickest point. 3. Remove the chops from the air fryer and allow them to rest for 5 minutes before serving.

Chorizo and Beef Burger

Prep time: 10 minutes | Cook time: 15 minutes | Serves 4

340 g 80/20 beef mince	chopped
110 g Mexican-style chorizo	2 teaspoons chili powder
crumb	1 teaspoon minced garlic
60 ml chopped onion	¼ teaspoon cumin
5 slices pickled jalapeños,	

1. In a large bowl, mix all ingredients. Divide the mixture into four sections and form them into burger patties. 2. Place burger patties into the air fryer basket, working in batches if necessary. 3. Adjust the temperature to 192°C and air fry for 15 minutes. 4. Flip the patties halfway through the cooking time. Serve warm.

Steak, Broccoli, and Mushroom Rice Bowls

Prep time: 10 minutes | Cook time: 15 to 18 minutes | Serves 4

2 tablespoons cornflour	1 onion, chopped
120 ml low-sodium beef stock	235 ml sliced white or chestnut
1 teaspoon reduced-salt soy	mushrooms
sauce	1 tablespoon grated peeled
340 g rump steak, cut into	fresh ginger
1-inch cubes	Cooked brown rice (optional),
120 ml broccoli florets	for serving

1. In a medium bowl, stir together the cornflour, beef stock, and soy sauce until the cornflour is completely dissolved. 2. Add the beef cubes and toss to coat. Let stand for 5 minutes at room temperature. 3. Insert the crisper plate into the basket and the basket into the unit. Preheat the unit by selecting AIR FRY, setting the temperature to 204°C, and setting the time to 3 minutes. Select START/STOP to begin. 4. Once the unit is preheated, use a slotted spoon to transfer the beef from the stock mixture into a medium metal bowl that fits into the basket. Reserve the stock. Add the broccoli, onion, mushrooms, and ginger to the beef. Place the bowl into the basket. 5. Select AIR FRY, set the temperature to 204°C, and set the time to 18 minutes. Select START/STOP to begin. 6. After about 12 minutes, check the beef and broccoli. If a food thermometer inserted into the beef registers at least 64°C and the vegetables are tender, add the reserved stock and resume cooking for about 3 minutes until the sauce boils. If not, resume cooking for about 3 minutes before adding the reservedstock. 7. When the cooking is complete, serve immediately over hot cooked brown rice, if desired.

Rosemary Ribeye Steaks

Prep time: 10 minutes | Cook time: 15 minutes | Serves 2

60 ml butter	1½ tablespoons balsamic
1 clove garlic, minced	vinegar
Salt and ground black pepper,	60 ml rosemary, chopped
to taste	2 ribeye steaks

1. Melt the butter in a skillet over medium heat. Add the garlic and fry until fragrant. 2. Remove the skillet from the heat and add the salt, pepper, and vinegar. Allow it to cool. 3. Add the rosemary, then pour the mixture into a Ziploc bag. 4. Put the ribeye steaks in the bag and shake well, coating the meat well. Refrigerate for an hour, then allow to sit for a further twenty minutes. 5. Preheat the air fryer to 204°C. 6. Air fry the ribeye steaks for 15 minutes. 7. Take care when removing the steaks from the air fryer and plate up. 8. Serve immediately.

Onion Pork Kebabs

Prep time: 22 minutes | Cook time: 18 minutes | Serves 3

2 tablespoons tomato purée	3 cloves garlic, peeled and
½ fresh green chilli, minced	finely minced
⅓ teaspoon paprika	1 teaspoon ground black
450 g pork mince	pepper, or more to taste
120 ml spring onions, finely	1 teaspoon salt, or more to taste
chopped	

1. Thoroughly combine all ingredients in a mixing dish. Then form your mixture into sausage shapes. 2. Cook for 18 minutes at 179°C. Mound salad on a serving platter, top with air-fried kebabs and serve warm. Bon appétit!

Spice-Rubbed Pork Loin

Prep time: 5 minutes | Cook time: 20 minutes | Serves 6

1 teaspoon paprika
½ teaspoon ground cumin
½ teaspoon chili powder
½ teaspoon garlic powder
2 tablespoons coconut oil

1 (680 g) boneless pork loin
½ teaspoon salt
¼ teaspoon ground black
pepper

1. In a small bowl, mix paprika, cumin, chili powder, and garlic powder. 2. Drizzle coconut oil over pork. Sprinkle pork loin with salt and pepper, then rub spice mixture evenly on all sides. 3. Place pork loin into ungreased air fryer basket. Adjust the temperature to 204°C and air fry for 20 minutes, turning pork halfway through cooking. Pork loin will be browned and have an internal temperature of at least 64°C when done. Serve warm.

Bo Luc Lac

Prep time: 50 minutes | Cook time: 8 minutes | Serves 4

For the Meat:
2 teaspoons soy sauce
4 garlic cloves, minced
1 teaspoon coarse or flaky salt
2 teaspoons sugar
¼ teaspoon ground black
pepper
1 teaspoon toasted sesame oil
680 g top rump steak, cut into
1-inch cubes
Cooking spray
For the Salad:
1 head butterhead lettuce,
leaves separated and torn into
large pieces
60 ml fresh mint leaves

120 ml halved baby plum
tomatoes
½ red onion, halved and thinly
sliced
2 tablespoons apple cider
vinegar
1 garlic clove, minced
2 teaspoons sugar
¼ teaspoon coarse or flaky salt
¼ teaspoon ground black
pepper
2 tablespoons vegetable oil
For Serving:
Lime wedges, for garnish
Coarse salt and freshly cracked
black pepper, to taste

1. Combine the ingredients for the meat, except for the steak, in a large bowl. Stir to mix well. 2. Dunk the steak cubes in the bowl and press to coat. Wrap the bowl in plastic and marinate under room temperature for at least 30 minutes. 3. Preheat the air fryer to 232°C. Spritz the air fryer basket with cooking spray. 4. Discard the marinade and transfer the steak cubes in the preheated air fryer basket. You need to air fry in batches to avoid overcrowding. 5. Air fry for 4 minutes or until the steak cubes are lightly browned but still have a little pink. Shake the basket halfway through the cooking time. 6. Meanwhile, combine the ingredients for the salad in a separate large bowl. Toss to mix well. 7. Pour the salad in a large serving bowl and top with the steak cubes. Squeeze the lime wedges over and sprinkle with salt and black pepper before serving.

Pork Kebab with Yogurt Sauce

Prep time: 25 minutes | Cook time: 12 minutes | Serves 4

2 teaspoons olive oil
230 g pork mince
230 g beef mince
1 egg, whisked
Sea salt and ground black
pepper, to taste
1 teaspoon paprika
2 garlic cloves, minced
1 teaspoon dried marjoram
1 teaspoon mustard seeds

½ teaspoon celery salt
Yogurt Sauce:
2 tablespoons olive oil
2 tablespoons fresh lemon juice
Sea salt, to taste
¼ teaspoon red pepper flakes,
crushed
120 ml full-fat yogurt
1 teaspoon dried dill

1. Spritz the sides and bottom of the air fryer basket with 2 teaspoons of olive oil. 2. In a mixing dish, thoroughly combine the pork, beef, egg, salt, black pepper, paprika, garlic, marjoram, mustard seeds, and celery salt. 3. Form the mixture into kebabs and transfer them to the greased basket. Cook at 185°C for 11 to 12 minutes, turning them over once or twice. In the meantime, mix all the sauce ingredients and place in the refrigerator until ready to serve. Serve the pork kebabs with the yogurt sauce on the side. Enjoy!

Parmesan-Crusted Steak

Prep time: 30 minutes | Cook time: 12 minutes | Serves 6

120 ml (1 stick) unsalted butter,
at room temperature
235 ml finely grated Parmesan
cheese
60 ml finely ground blanched

almond flour
680 g sirloin steak
Sea salt and freshly ground
black pepper, to taste

1. Place the butter, Parmesan cheese, and almond flour in a food processor. Process until smooth. Transfer to a sheet of parchment paper and form into a log. Wrap tightly in plastic wrap. Freeze for 45 minutes or refrigerate for at least 4 hours. 2. While the butter is chilling, season the steak liberally with salt and pepper. Let the steak rest at room temperature for about 45 minutes. 3. Place the grill pan or basket in your air fryer, set it to 204°C, and let it preheat for 5 minutes. 4. Working in batches, if necessary, place the steak on the grill pan and air fry for 4 minutes. Flip and cook for 3 minutes more, until the steak is brown on both sides. 5. Remove the steak from the air fryer and arrange an equal amount of the Parmesan butter on top of each steak. Return the steak to the air fryer and continue cooking for another 5 minutes, until an instant-read thermometer reads 49°C for medium-rare and the crust is golden brown (or to your desired doneness). 6. Transfer the cooked steak to a plate; let rest for 10 minutes before serving.

Spicy Tomato Beef Meatballs

Prep time: 10 minutes | Cook time: 15 minutes | Serves 4

3 spring onions, minced	taste
1 garlic clove, minced	450 g 95% lean beef mince
1 egg yolk	Olive oil spray
60 ml cream cracker crumbs	300 ml any tomato pasta sauce
Pinch salt	2 tablespoons Dijon mustard
Freshly ground black pepper, to	

1. In a large bowl, combine the spring onionspring onions, garlic, egg yolk, cracker crumbs, salt, and pepper and mix well. 2. Add the beef and gently but thoroughly mix with your hands until combined. Form the meat mixture into 1½-inch round meatballs. 3. Insert the crisper plate into the basket and the basket into the unit. Preheat the unit by selecting BAKE, setting the temperature to 204°C, and setting the time to 3 minutes. Select START/STOP to begin. 4. Once the unit is preheated, spray the crisper plate with olive oil. Working in batches, spray the meatballs with olive oil and place them into the basket in a single layer, without touching. 5. Select BAKE, set the temperature to 204°C, and set the time to 11 minutes. Select START/STOP to begin. 6. When the cooking is complete, a food thermometer inserted into the meatballs should register 74°C. Transfer the meatballs to a 6-inch metal bowl. 7. Repeat steps 4, 5, and 6 with the remaining meatballs. 8. Top the meatballs with the pasta sauce and Dijon mustard, and mix gently. Place the bowl into the basket. 9. Select BAKE, set the temperature to 204°C, and set the time to 4 minutes. Select START/STOP to begin. 10. When the cooking is complete, serve hot.

Ritzy Skirt Steak Fajitas

Prep time: 15 minutes | Cook time: 30 minutes | Serves 4

2 tablespoons olive oil	1 green pepper, sliced
60 ml lime juice	Salt and freshly ground black
1 clove garlic, minced	pepper, to taste
½ teaspoon ground cumin	8 flour tortillas
½ teaspoon hot sauce	Toppings:
½ teaspoon salt	Shredded lettuce
2 tablespoons chopped fresh	Crumbled feta or ricotta (or
coriander	grated Cheddar cheese)
450 g skirt steak	Sliced black olives
1 onion, sliced	Diced tomatoes
1 teaspoon chili powder	Sour cream
1 red pepper, sliced	Guacamole

1. Combine the olive oil, lime juice, garlic, cumin, hot sauce, salt and coriander in a shallow dish. Add the skirt steak and turn it over several times to coat all sides. Pierce the steak with a needle-style meat tenderizer or paring knife. Marinate the steak in the refrigerator for at least 3 hours, or overnight. When you are ready to cook, remove the steak from the refrigerator and let it sit at room temperature for 30 minutes. 2. Preheat the air fryer to 204°C. 3. Toss the onion slices with the chili powder and a little olive oil and transfer them to the air fryer basket. Air fry for 5 minutes. Add the red and green peppers to the air fryer basket with the onions, season with salt and pepper and air fry for 8 more minutes, until the onions and peppers are soft. Transfer the vegetables to a dish and cover with aluminum foil to keep warm. 4. Put the skirt steak in the air fryer basket and pour the marinade over the top. Air fry at 204°C for 12 minutes. Flip the steak over and air fry for an additional 5 minutes. Transfer the cooked steak to a cutting board and let the steak rest for a few minutes. If the peppers and onions need to be heated, return them to the air fryer for just 1 to 2 minutes. 5. Thinly slice the steak at an angle, cutting against the grain of the steak. Serve the steak with the onions and peppers, the warm tortillas and the fajita toppings on the side.

Simple Beef Mince with Courgette

Prep time: 5 minutes | Cook time: 12 minutes | Serves 4

680 g beef mince	1 teaspoon dried basil
450 g chopped courgette	1 teaspoon dried rosemary
2 tablespoons extra-virgin olive	2 tablespoons fresh chives,
oil	chopped
1 teaspoon dried oregano	

1. Preheat the air fryer to 204°C. 2. In a large bowl, combine all the ingredients, except for the chives, until well blended. 3. Place the beef and courgette mixture in the baking pan. Air fry for 12 minutes, or until the beef is browned and the courgette is tender. 4. Divide the beef and courgette mixture among four serving dishes. Top with fresh chives and serve hot.

Cheddar Bacon Burst with Spinach

Prep time: 5 minutes | Cook time: 60 minutes | Serves 8

30 slices bacon	2 teaspoons Italian seasoning
1 tablespoon Chipotle chilli	120 ml Cheddar cheese
powder	1 L raw spinach

1. Preheat the air fryer to 192°C. 2. Weave the bacon into 15 vertical pieces and 12 horizontal pieces. Cut the extra 3 in half to fill in the rest, horizontally. 3. Season the bacon with Chipotle chilli powder and Italian seasoning. 4. Add the cheese to the bacon. 5. Add the spinach and press down to compress. 6. Tightly roll up the woven bacon. 7. Line a baking sheet with kitchen foil and add plenty of salt to it. 8. Put the bacon on top of a cooling rack and put that on top of the baking sheet. 9. Bake for 60 minutes. 10. Let cool for 15 minutes before slicing and serving.

Mustard Herb Pork Tenderloin

Prep time: 5 minutes | Cook time: 20 minutes | Serves 6

60 ml mayonnaise	1 (450 g) pork tenderloin
2 tablespoons Dijon mustard	½ teaspoon salt
½ teaspoon dried thyme	¼ teaspoon ground black
¼ teaspoon dried rosemary	pepper

1. In a small bowl, mix mayonnaise, mustard, thyme, and rosemary. Brush tenderloin with mixture on all sides, then sprinkle with salt and pepper on all sides. 2. Place tenderloin into ungreased air fryer basket. Adjust the temperature to 204°C and air fry for 20 minutes, turning tenderloin halfway through cooking. Tenderloin will be golden and have an internal temperature of at least 64°C when done. Serve warm.

Mexican Pork Chops

Prep time: 5 minutes | Cook time: 15 minutes | Serves 2

¼ teaspoon dried oregano	2 (110 g) boneless pork chops
1½ teaspoons taco seasoning or	2 tablespoons unsalted butter,
fajita seasoning mix	divided

1. Preheat the air fryer to 204°C. 2. Combine the dried oregano and taco seasoning in a small bowl and rub the mixture into the pork chops. Brush the chops with 1 tablespoon butter. 3. In the air fryer, air fry the chops for 15 minutes, turning them over halfway through to air fry on the other side. 4. When the chops are a brown color, check the internal temperature has reached 64°C and remove from the air fryer. Serve with a garnish of remaining butter.

Beefy Poppers

Prep time: 15 minutes | Cook time: 15 minutes | Makes 8 poppers

8 medium jalapeño peppers, stemmed, halved, and seeded	1 teaspoon fine sea salt
1 (230 g) package cream cheese (or cream cheese style spread for dairy-free), softened	½ teaspoon ground black pepper
	8 slices thin-cut bacon
900 g beef mince (85% lean)	Fresh coriander leaves, for garnish

1. Spray the air fryer basket with avocado oil. Preheat the air fryer to 204°C. 2. Stuff each jalapeño half with a few tablespoons of cream cheese. Place the halves back together again to form 8 jalapeños. 3. Season the beef mince with the salt and pepper and mix with your hands to incorporate. Flatten about 110 g of beef in the palm of your hand and place a stuffed jalapeño in the center. Fold the beef around the jalapeño, forming an egg shape. Wrap the beef-covered jalapeño with a slice of bacon and secure it with a toothpick. 4. Place the jalapeños in the air fryer basket, leaving space between them (if you're using a smaller air fryer, work in batches if necessary), and air fry for 15 minutes, or until the beef is cooked through and the bacon is crispy. Garnish with coriander before serving. 5. Store leftovers in an airtight container in the fridge for 3 days or in the freezer for up to a month. Reheat in a preheated 176°C air fryer for 4 minutes, or until heated through and the bacon is crispy.

Zesty London Broil

Prep time: 30 minutes | Cook time: 20 to 28 minutes | Serves 4 to 6

160 ml ketchup	2 tablespoons minced onion
60 ml honey	½ teaspoon paprika
60 ml olive oil	1 teaspoon salt
2 tablespoons apple cider vinegar	1 teaspoon freshly ground black pepper
2 tablespoons Worcestershire sauce	900 g bavette or skirt steak (about 1-inch thick)

1. Combine the ketchup, honey, olive oil, apple cider vinegar, Worcestershire sauce, minced onion, paprika, salt and pepper in a small bowl and whisk together. 2. Generously pierce both sides of the meat with a fork or meat tenderizer and place it in a shallow dish. Pour the marinade mixture over the steak, making sure all sides of the meat get coated with the marinade. Cover and refrigerate overnight. 3. Preheat the air fryer to 204°C. 4. Transfer the steak to the air fryer basket and air fry for 20 to 28 minutes, depending on how rare or well done you like your steak. Flip the steak over halfway through the cooking time. 5. Remove the steak from the air fryer and let it rest for five minutes on a cutting board. To serve, thinly slice the meat against the grain and transfer to a serving platter.

Italian Pork Loin

Prep time: 30 minutes | Cook time: 16 minutes | Serves 3

1 teaspoon sea salt	2 garlic cloves, minced
½ teaspoon black pepper, freshly cracked	450 g pork loin joint
60 ml red wine	1 tablespoon Italian herb seasoning blend
2 tablespoons mustard	

1. In a ceramic bowl, mix the salt, black pepper, red wine, mustard, and garlic. Add the pork loin and let it marinate at least 30 minutes. 2. Spritz the sides and bottom of the air fryer basket with nonstick cooking spray. 3. Place the pork loin in the basket; sprinkle with the Italian herb seasoning blend. Cook the pork loin at 188°C for 10 minutes. Flip halfway through, spraying with cooking oil and cook for 5 to 6 minutes more. Serve immediately.

Stuffed Beef Fillet with Feta Cheese

Prep time: 10 minutes | Cook time: 10 minutes | Serves 4

680 g beef fillet, pounded to ¼ inch thick	120 ml crumbled feta cheese
3 teaspoons sea salt	60 ml finely chopped onions
1 teaspoon ground black pepper	2 cloves garlic, minced
60 g creamy goat cheese	Cooking spray

1. Preheat the air fryer to 204°C. Spritz the air fryer basket with cooking spray. 2. Unfold the beef on a clean work surface. Rub the salt and pepper all over the beef to season. 3. Make the filling for the stuffed beef fillet: Combine the goat cheese, feta, onions, and garlic in a medium bowl. Stir until well blended. 4. Spoon the mixture in the center of the fillet. Roll the fillet up tightly like rolling a burrito and use some kitchen twine to tie the fillet. 5. Arrange the fillet in the air fryer basket and air fry for 10 minutes, flipping the fillet halfway through to ensure even cooking, or until an instant-read thermometer inserted in the center of the fillet registers 57°C for medium-rare. 6. Transfer to a platter and serve immediately.

Sesame Beef Lettuce Tacos

Prep time: 30 minutes | Cook time: 8 to 10 minutes | Serves 4

60 ml soy sauce or tamari	450 g bavette or skirt steak
60 ml avocado oil	8 butterhead lettuce leaves
2 tablespoons cooking sherry	2 spring onions, sliced
1 tablespoon granulated sweetener	1 tablespoon toasted sesame seeds
1 tablespoon ground cumin	Hot sauce, for serving
1 teaspoon minced garlic	Lime wedges, for serving
Sea salt and freshly ground black pepper, to taste	Flaky sea salt (optional)

1. In a small bowl, whisk together the soy sauce, avocado oil, cooking sherry, sweetener, cumin, garlic, and salt and pepper to taste. 2. Place the steak in a shallow dish. Pour the marinade over the beef. Cover the dish with plastic wrap and let it marinate in the refrigerator for at least 2 hours or overnight. 3. Remove the flank steak from the dish and discard the marinade. 4. Set the air fryer to 204°C. Place the steak in the air fryer basket and air fry for 4 to 6 minutes. Flip the steak and cook for 4 minutes more, until an instant-read thermometer reads 49°C at the thickest part (or cook it to your desired doneness). Allow the steak to rest for 10 minutes, then slice it thinly against the grain. 5. Stack 2 lettuce leaves on top of each other and add some sliced meat. Top with spring onions and sesame seeds. Drizzle with hot sauce and lime juice, and finish with a little flaky salt (if using). Repeat with the remaining lettuce leaves and fillings.

Green Pepper Cheeseburgers

Prep time: 5 minutes | Cook time: 30 minutes | Serves 4

2 green peppers	black pepper
680 g 85% lean beef mince	4 slices Cheddar cheese (about 85 g)
1 clove garlic, minced	4 large lettuce leaves
1 teaspoon salt	
½ teaspoon freshly ground	

1. Preheat the air fryer to 204°C. 2. Arrange the peppers in the basket of the air fryer. Pausing halfway through the cooking time to turn the peppers, air fry for 20 minutes, or until they are softened and beginning to char. Transfer the peppers to a large bowl and cover with a plate. When cool enough to handle, peel off the skin, remove the seeds and stems, and slice into strips. Set aside. 3. Meanwhile, in a large bowl, combine the beef with the garlic, salt, and pepper. Shape the beef into 4 patties. 4. Lower the heat on the air fryer to 182°C. Arrange the burgers in a single layer in the basket of the air fryer. Pausing halfway through the cooking time to turn the burgers, air fry for 10 minutes, or until a thermometer inserted into the thickest part registers 72°C. 5. Top the burgers with the cheese slices and continue baking for a minute or two, just until the cheese has melted. Serve the burgers on a lettuce leaf topped with the roasted peppers.

Cheese Wine Pork Loin

Prep time: 30 minutes | Cook time: 15 minutes | Serves 2

235 ml water	½ teaspoon porcini powder
235 ml red wine	Sea salt and ground black
1 tablespoon sea salt	pepper, to taste
2 pork loin steaks	1 egg
60 ml ground almonds	60 ml yoghurt
60 ml flaxseed meal	1 teaspoon wholegrain or
½ teaspoon baking powder	English mustard
1 teaspoon onion granules	80 ml Parmesan cheese, grated

1. In a large ceramic dish, combine the water, wine and salt. Add the pork and put for 1 hour in the refrigerator. 2. In a shallow bowl, mix the ground almonds, flaxseed meal, baking powder, onion granules, porcini powder, salt, and ground pepper. In another bowl, whisk the eggs with yoghurt and mustard. 3. In a third bowl, place the grated Parmesan cheese. 4. Dip the pork in the seasoned flour mixture and toss evenly; then, in the egg mixture. Finally, roll them over the grated Parmesan cheese. 5. Spritz the bottom of the air fryer basket with cooking oil. Add the breaded pork and cook at 202°C and for 10 minutes. 6. Flip and cook for 5 minutes more on the other side. Serve warm.

Easy Lamb Chops with Asparagus

Prep time: 10 minutes | Cook time: 15 minutes | Serves 4

4 asparagus spears, trimmed
2 tablespoons olive oil, divided
450 g lamb chops
1 garlic clove, minced

2 teaspoons chopped fresh thyme, for serving
Salt and ground black pepper, to taste

1. Preheat the air fryer to 204°C. Spritz the air fryer basket with cooking spray. 2. On a large plate, brush the asparagus with 1 tablespoon olive oil, then sprinkle with salt. Set aside. 3. On a separate plate, brush the lamb chops with remaining olive oil and sprinkle with salt and ground black pepper. 4. Arrange the lamb chops in the preheated air fryer. Air fry for 10 minutes. 5. Flip the lamb chops and add the asparagus and garlic. Air fry for 5 more minutes or until the lamb is well browned and the asparagus is tender. 6. Serve them on a plate with thyme on top.

Sumptuous Pizza Tortilla Rolls

Prep time: 10 minutes | Cook time: 6 minutes | Serves 4

1 teaspoon butter
½ medium onion, slivered
½ red or green pepper, julienned
110 g fresh white mushrooms, chopped
120 ml pizza sauce

8 flour tortillas
8 thin slices wafer-thinham
24 pepperoni slices
235 ml shredded Mozzarella cheese
Cooking spray

1. Preheat the air fryer to 200°C. 2. Put butter, onions, pepper, and mushrooms in a baking pan. Bake in the preheated air fryer for 3 minutes. Stir and cook 3 to 4 minutes longer until just crisp and tender. Remove pan and set aside. 3. To assemble rolls, spread about 2 teaspoons of pizza sauce on one half of each tortilla. Top with a slice of ham and 3 slices of pepperoni. Divide sautéed vegetables among tortillas and top with cheese. 4. Roll up tortillas, secure with toothpicks if needed, and spray with oil. 5. Put 4 rolls in air fryer basket and air fry for 4 minutes. Turn and air fry 4 minutes, until heated through and lightly browned. 6. Repeat step 4 to air fry remaining pizza rolls. 7. Serve immediately.

Sirloin Steak with Honey-Mustard Butter

Prep time: 5 minutes | Cook time: 14 minutes | Serves 4

900 g beef sirloin steak
1 teaspoon cayenne pepper
1 tablespoon honey
1 tablespoon Dijon mustard

½ stick butter, softened
Sea salt and freshly ground black pepper, to taste
Cooking spray

1. Preheat the air fryer to 204°C and spritz with cooking spray. 2. Sprinkle the steak with cayenne pepper, salt, and black pepper on a clean work surface. 3. Arrange the steak in the preheated air fryer and spritz with cooking spray. 4. Air fry for 14 minutes or until browned and reach your desired doneness. Flip the steak halfway through. 5. Meanwhile, combine the honey, mustard, and butter in a small bowl. Stir to mix well. 6. Transfer the air fried steak onto a plate and baste with the honey-mustard butter before serving.

Mojito Lamb Chops

Prep time: 30 minutes | Cook time: 5 minutes | Serves 2

Marinade:
2 teaspoons grated lime zest
120 ml lime juice
60 ml avocado oil
60 ml chopped fresh mint leaves
4 cloves garlic, roughly chopped

2 teaspoons fine sea salt
½ teaspoon ground black pepper
4 (1-inch-thick) lamb chops
Sprigs of fresh mint, for garnish (optional)
Lime slices, for serving (optional)

1. Make the marinade: Place all the ingredients for the marinade in a food processor or blender and purée until mostly smooth with a few small chunks. Transfer half of the marinade to a shallow dish and set the other half aside for serving. Add the lamb to the shallow dish, cover, and place in the refrigerator to marinate for at least 2 hours or overnight. 2. Spray the air fryer basket with avocado oil. Preheat the air fryer to 200°C. 3. Remove the chops from the marinade and place them in the air fryer basket. Air fry for 5 minutes, or until the internal temperature reaches 64°C for medium doneness. 4. Allow the chops to rest for 10 minutes before serving with the rest of the marinade as a sauce. Garnish with fresh mint leaves and serve with lime slices, if desired. Best served fresh.

Fillet with Crispy Shallots

Prep time: 30 minutes | Cook time: 18 to 20 minutes | Serves 6

680 g beef fillet steaks
Sea salt and freshly ground black pepper, to taste

4 medium shallots
1 teaspoon olive oil or avocado oil

1. Season both sides of the steaks with salt and pepper, and let them sit at room temperature for 45 minutes. 2. Set the air fryer to 204°C and let it preheat for 5 minutes. 3. Working in batches if necessary, place the steaks in the air fryer basket in a single layer and air fry for 5 minutes. Flip and cook for 5 minutes longer, until an instant-read thermometer inserted in the center of the steaks registers 49°C for medium-rare (or as desired). Remove the steaks and tent with aluminum foil to rest. 4. Set the air fryer to 149°C. In a medium bowl, toss the shallots with the oil. Place the shallots in the basket and air fry for 5 minutes, then give them a toss and cook for 3 to 5 minutes more, until crispy and golden brown. 5. Place the steaks on serving plates and arrange the shallots on top.

Sausage and Cauliflower Arancini

Prep time: 30 minutes | Cook time: 28 to 32 minutes | Serves 6

Avocado oil spray	85 g cream cheese
170 g Italian-seasoned sausage, casings removed	110 g Cheddar cheese, shredded
60 ml diced onion	1 large egg
1 teaspoon minced garlic	120 ml finely ground blanched almond flour
1 teaspoon dried thyme	60 ml finely grated Parmesan cheese
Sea salt and freshly ground black pepper, to taste	Keto-friendly marinara sauce, for serving
120 ml cauliflower rice	

1. Spray a large skillet with oil and place it over medium-high heat. Once the skillet is hot, put the sausage in the skillet and cook for 7 minutes, breaking up the meat with the back of a spoon. 2. Reduce the heat to medium and add the onion. Cook for 5 minutes, then add the garlic, thyme, and salt and pepper to taste. Cook for 1 minute more. 3. Add the cauliflower rice and cream cheese to the skillet. Cook for 7 minutes, stirring frequently, until the cream cheese melts and the cauliflower is tender. 4. Remove the skillet from the heat and stir in the Cheddar cheese. Using a cookie scoop, form the mixture into 1½-inch balls. Place the balls on a parchment paper-lined baking sheet. Freeze for 30 minutes. 5. Place the egg in a shallow bowl and beat it with a fork. In a separate bowl, stir together the almond flour and Parmesan cheese. 6. Dip the cauliflower balls into the egg, then coat them with the almond flour mixture, gently pressing the mixture to the balls to adhere. 7. Set the air fryer to 204°C. Spray the cauliflower rice balls with oil, and arrange them in a single layer in the air fryer basket, working in batches if necessary. Air fry for 5 minutes. Flip the rice balls and spray them with more oil. Air fry for 3 to 7 minutes longer, until the balls are golden brown. 8. Serve warm with marinara sauce.

Italian Lamb Chops with Avocado Mayo

Prep time: 5 minutes | Cook time: 12 minutes | Serves 2

2 lamp chops	120 ml mayonnaise
2 teaspoons Italian herbs	1 tablespoon lemon juice
2 avocados	

1. Season the lamb chops with the Italian herbs, then set aside for 5 minutes. 2. Preheat the air fryer to 204°C and place the rack inside. 3. Put the chops on the rack and air fry for 12 minutes. 4. In the meantime, halve the avocados and open to remove the pits. Spoon the flesh into a blender. 5. Add the mayonnaise and lemon juice and pulse until a smooth consistency is achieved. 6. Take care when removing the chops from the air fryer, then plate up and serve with the avocado mayo.

Pork Schnitzels with Sour Cream and Dill Sauce

Prep time: 5 minutes | Cook time: 24 minutes | Serves 4 to 6

120 ml flour	2 tablespoons olive oil
1½ teaspoons salt	3 tablespoons melted butter
Freshly ground black pepper, to taste	Lemon wedges, for serving
2 eggs	Sour Cream and Dill Sauce:
120 ml milk	235 ml chicken stock
355 ml toasted breadcrumbs	1½ tablespoons cornflour
1 teaspoon paprika	80 ml sour cream
6 boneless pork chops (about 680 g), fat trimmed, pound to ½-inch thick	1½ tablespoons chopped fresh dill
	Salt and ground black pepper, to taste

1. Preheat the air fryer to 204°C. 2. Combine the flour with salt and black pepper in a large bowl. Stir to mix well. Whisk the egg with milk in a second bowl. Stir the breadcrumbs and paprika in a third bowl. 3. Dredge the pork chops in the flour bowl, then in the egg milk, and then into the breadcrumbs bowl. Press to coat well. Shake the excess off. 4. Arrange one pork chop in the preheated air fryer each time, then brush with olive oil and butter on all sides. 5. Air fry each pork chop for 4 minutes or until golden brown and crispy. Flip the chop halfway through the cooking time. 6. Transfer the cooked pork chop (schnitzel) to a baking pan in the oven and keep warm over low heat while air frying the remaining pork chops. 7. Meanwhile, combine the chicken stock and cornflour in a small saucepan and bring to a boil over medium-high heat. Simmer for 2 more minutes. 8. Turn off the heat, then mix in the sour cream, fresh dill, salt, and black pepper. 9. Remove the schnitzels from the air fryer to a plate and baste with sour cream and dill sauce. Squeeze the lemon wedges over and slice to serve.

Peppercorn-Crusted Beef Fillet

Prep time: 10 minutes | Cook time: 25 minutes | Serves 6

2 tablespoons salted butter, melted	3 tablespoons ground 4-peppercorn blend
2 teaspoons minced roasted garlic	1 (900 g) beef fillet, trimmed of visible fat

1. In a small bowl, mix the butter and roasted garlic. Brush it over the beef fillet. 2. Place the ground peppercorns onto a plate and roll the fillet through them, creating a crust. Place fillet into the air fryer basket. 3. Adjust the temperature to 204°C and roast for 25 minutes. 4. Turn the fillet halfway through the cooking time. 5. Allow meat to rest 10 minutes before slicing.

Broccoli and Pork Teriyaki

Prep time: 10 minutes | Cook time: 13 minutes | Serves 4

1 head broccoli, trimmed into florets	450 g pork tenderloin, trimmed and cut into 1-inch pieces
1 tablespoon extra-virgin olive oil	120 ml teriyaki sauce, divided
¼ teaspoon sea salt	Olive oil spray
¼ teaspoon freshly ground black pepper	475 ml cooked brown rice
	Sesame seeds, for garnish

1. Insert the crisper plate into the basket and the basket into the unit. Preheat the unit by selecting AIR ROAST, setting the temperature to 204ºC, and setting the time to 3 minutes. Select START/STOP to begin. 2. In a large bowl, toss together the broccoli, olive oil, salt, and pepper. 3. In a medium bowl, toss together the pork and 3 tablespoons of teriyaki sauce to coat the meat. 4. Once the unit is preheated, spray the crisper plate with olive oil. Put the broccoli and pork into the basket. Spray them with olive oil and drizzle with 1 tablespoon of teriyaki sauce. 5. Select AIR ROAST, set the temperature to 204ºC, and set the time to 13 minutes. Select START/STOP to begin. 6. After 10 to 12 minutes, the broccoli is tender and light golden brown and a food thermometer inserted into the pork should register 64ºC. Remove the basket and drizzle the broccoli and pork with the remaining 60 ml of teriyaki sauce and toss to coat. Reinsert the basket to resume cooking for 1 minute. 7. When the cooking is complete, serve immediately over the hot cooked rice, if desired, garnished with the sesame seeds.

Vietnamese "Shaking" Beef

Prep time: 30 minutes | Cook time: 4 minutes per batch | Serves 4

Meat:	¼ teaspoon coarse or flaky salt
4 garlic cloves, minced	¼ teaspoon black pepper
2 teaspoons soy sauce	½ red onion, halved and very thinly sliced
2 teaspoons sugar	
1 teaspoon toasted sesame oil	1 head butterhead lettuce, leaves separated and torn into large pieces
1 teaspoon coarse or flaky salt	
¼ teaspoon black pepper	
680 g flat iron or top rump steak, cut into 1-inch cubes	120 ml halved baby plum tomatoes
Salad:	60 ml fresh mint leaves
2 tablespoons rice vinegar or apple cider vinegar	For Serving:
	Lime wedges
2 tablespoons vegetable oil	Coarse salt and freshly cracked black pepper, to taste
1 garlic clove, minced	
2 teaspoons sugar	

1. For the meat: In a small bowl, combine the garlic, soy sauce, sugar, sesame oil, salt, and pepper. Place the meat in a gallon-size resealable plastic bag. Pour the marinade over the meat. Seal and place the bag in a large bowl. Marinate for 30 minutes, or cover and refrigerate for up to 24 hours. 2. Place half the meat in the air fryer basket. Set the air fryer to 232ºC for 4 minutes, shaking the basket to redistribute the meat halfway through the cooking time. Transfer the meat to a plate (it should be medium-rare, still pink in the middle). Cover lightly with aluminum foil. Repeat to cook the remaining meat. 3. Meanwhile, for the salad: In a large bowl, whisk together the vinegar, vegetable oil, garlic, sugar, salt, and pepper. Add the onion. Stir to combine. Add the lettuce, tomatoes, and mint and toss to combine. Arrange the salad on a serving platter. 4. Arrange the cooked meat over the salad. Drizzle any accumulated juices from the plate over the meat. Serve with lime wedges, coarse salt, and cracked black pepper.

Bacon, Cheese and Pear Stuffed Pork

Prep time: 10 minutes | Cook time: 24 minutes | Serves 3

4 slices bacon, chopped	⅛ teaspoon black pepper
1 tablespoon butter	1 pear, finely diced
120 ml finely diced onion	80 ml crumbled blue cheese
80 ml chicken stock	3 boneless pork chops (2-inch thick)
355 ml seasoned stuffing mix	
1 egg, beaten	Olive oil
½ teaspoon dried thyme	Salt and freshly ground black pepper, to taste
½ teaspoon salt	

1. Preheat the air fryer to 204ºC. 2. Place the bacon into the air fryer basket and air fry for 6 minutes, stirring halfway through the cooking time. Remove the bacon and set it aside on a paper towel. Pour out the grease from the bottom of the air fryer. 3. Make the stuffing: Melt the butter in a medium saucepan over medium heat on the stovetop. Add the onion and sauté for a few minutes, until it starts to soften. Add the chicken stock and simmer for 1 minute. Remove the pan from the heat and add the stuffing mix. Stir until the stock has been absorbed. Add the egg, dried thyme, salt and freshly ground black pepper, and stir until combined. Fold in the diced pear and crumbled blue cheese. 4. Place the pork chops on a cutting board. Using the palm of your hand to hold the chop flat and steady, slice into the side of the pork chop to make a pocket in the center of the chop. Leave about an inch of chop uncut and make sure you don't cut all the way through the pork chop. Brush both sides of the pork chops with olive oil and season with salt and freshly ground black pepper. Stuff each pork chop with a third of the stuffing, packing the stuffing tightly inside the pocket. 5. Preheat the air fryer to 182ºC. 6. Spray or brush the sides of the air fryer basket with oil. Place the pork chops in the air fryer basket with the open stuffed edge of the pork chop facing the outside edges of the basket. 7. Air fry the pork chops for 18 minutes, turning the pork chops over halfway through the cooking time. When the chops are done, let them rest for 5 minutes and then transfer to a serving platter.

Smothered Chops

Prep time: 20 minutes | Cook time: 30 minutes | Serves 4

4 bone-in pork chops (230 g each)
2 teaspoons salt, divided
1½ teaspoons freshly ground black pepper, divided
1 teaspoon garlic powder
235 ml tomato purée
1½ teaspoons Italian seasoning
1 tablespoon sugar
1 tablespoon cornflour
120 ml chopped onion
120 ml chopped green pepper
1 to 2 tablespoons oil

1. Evenly season the pork chops with 1 teaspoon salt, 1 teaspoon pepper, and the garlic powder. 2. In a medium bowl, stir together the tomato purée, Italian seasoning, sugar, remaining 1 teaspoon of salt, and remaining ½ teaspoon of pepper. 3. In a small bowl, whisk 180 ml water and the cornflour until blended. Stir this slurry into the tomato purée, with the onion and green pepper. Transfer to a baking pan. 4. Preheat the air fryer to 176ºC. 5. Place the sauce in the fryer and cook for 10 minutes. Stir and cook for 10 minutes more. Remove the pan and keep warm. 6. Increase the air fryer temperature to 204ºC. Line the air fryer basket with parchment paper. 7. Place the pork chops on the parchment and spritz with oil. 8. Cook for 5 minutes. Flip and spritz the chops with oil and cook for 5 minutes more, until the internal temperature reaches 64ºC. Serve with the tomato mixture spooned on top.

Air Fried Beef Satay with Peanut Dipping Sauce

Prep time: 30 minutes | Cook time: 5 to 7 minutes | Serves 4

230 g bavette or skirt steak, sliced into 8 strips
2 teaspoons curry powder
½ teaspoon coarse or flaky salt
Cooking spray
Peanut Dipping sauce:
2 tablespoons creamy peanut butter
1 tablespoon reduced-salt soy
sauce
2 teaspoons rice vinegar
1 teaspoon honey
1 teaspoon grated ginger
Special Equipment:
4 bamboo skewers, cut into halves and soaked in water for 20 minutes to keep them from burning while cooking

1. Preheat the air fryer to 182ºC. Spritz the air fryer basket with cooking spray. 2. In a bowl, place the steak strips and sprinkle with the curry powder and coarse or flaky salt to season. Thread the strips onto the soaked skewers. 3. Arrange the skewers in the prepared air fryer basket and spritz with cooking spray. Air fry for 5 to 7 minutes, or until the beef is well browned, turning halfway through. 4. In the meantime, stir together the peanut butter, soy sauce, rice vinegar, honey, and ginger in a bowl to make the dipping sauce. 5. Transfer the beef to the serving dishes and let rest for 5 minutes. Serve with the peanut dipping sauce on the side.

Cajun Bacon Pork Loin Fillet

Prep time: 30 minutes | Cook time: 20 minutes | Serves 6

680 g pork loin fillet or pork tenderloin
3 tablespoons olive oil
2 tablespoons Cajun spice mix
Salt, to taste
6 slices bacon
Olive oil spray

1. Cut the pork in half so that it will fit in the air fryer basket. 2. Place both pieces of meat in a resealable plastic bag. Add the oil, Cajun seasoning, and salt to taste, if using. Seal the bag and massage to coat all of the meat with the oil and seasonings. Marinate in the refrigerator for at least 1 hour or up to 24 hours. 3. Remove the pork from the bag and wrap 3 bacon slices around each piece. Spray the air fryer basket with olive oil spray. Place the meat in the air fryer. Set the air fryer to 176ºC for 15 minutes. Increase the temperature to 204ºC for 5 minutes. Use a meat thermometer to ensure the meat has reached an internal temperature of 64ºC. 4. Let the meat rest for 10 minutes. Slice into 6 medallions and serve.

Greek Pork with Tzatziki Sauce

Prep time: 30 minutes | Cook time: 50 minutes | Serves 4

Greek Pork:
900 g pork loin roasting joint
Salt and black pepper, to taste
1 teaspoon smoked paprika
½ teaspoon mustard seeds
½ teaspoon celery salt
1 teaspoon fennel seeds
1 teaspoon chili powder
1 teaspoon turmeric powder
½ teaspoon ground ginger
2 tablespoons olive oil
2 cloves garlic, finely chopped
Tzatziki:
½ cucumber, finely chopped and squeezed
235 ml full-fat Greek yogurt
1 garlic clove, minced
1 tablespoon extra-virgin olive oil
1 teaspoon balsamic vinegar
1 teaspoon minced fresh dill
A pinch of salt

1. Toss all ingredients for Greek pork in a large mixing bowl. Toss until the meat is well coated. 2. Cook in the preheated air fryer at 182ºC for 30 minutes; turn over and cook another 20 minutes. 3. Meanwhile, prepare the tzatziki by mixing all the tzatziki ingredients. Place in your refrigerator until ready to use. 4. Serve the pork sirloin roast with the chilled tzatziki on the side. Enjoy!

Chapter 7 Vegetables and Sides

Buffalo Cauliflower with Blue Cheese

Prep time: 15 minutes | Cook time: 5 to 7 minutes per batch | Serves 6

1 large head cauliflower, rinsed and separated into small florets	190 g nonfat Greek yogurt
1 tablespoon extra-virgin olive oil	60 g buttermilk
	½ teaspoon hot sauce
½ teaspoon garlic powder	1 celery stalk, chopped
Cooking oil spray	2 tablespoons crumbled blue cheese
80 ml hot wing sauce	

1. Insert the crisper plate into the basket and the basket into the unit. Preheat the unit by selecting AIR FRY, setting the temperature to192ºC, and setting the time to 3 minutes. Select START/STOP to begin. 2. In a large bowl, toss together the cauliflower florets and olive oil. Sprinkle with the garlic powder and toss again to coat. 3. Once the unit is preheated, spray the crisper plate with cooking oil. Put half the cauliflower into the basket. 4. Select AIR FRY, set the temperature to192ºC, and set the time to 7 minutes. Select START/STOP to begin. 5. After 3 minutes, remove the basket and shake the cauliflower. Reinsert the basket to resume cooking. After 2 minutes, check the cauliflower. It is done when it is browned. If not, resume cooking. 6. When the cooking is complete, transfer the cauliflower to a serving bowl and toss with half the hot wing sauce. 7. Repeat steps 4, 5, and 6 with the remaining cauliflower and hot wing sauce. 8. In a small bowl, stir together the yogurt, buttermilk, hot sauce, celery, and blue cheese. Drizzle the sauce over the finished cauliflower and serve.

Cheese-Walnut Stuffed Mushrooms

Prep time: 5 minutes | Cook time: 10 minutes | Serves 4

4 large portobello mushrooms	35 g minced walnuts
1 tablespoon rapeseed oil	2 tablespoons chopped fresh parsley
110 g shredded Mozzarella cheese	Cooking spray

1. Preheat the air fryer to 180ºC. Spritz the air fryer basket with cooking spray. 2. On a clean work surface, remove the mushroom stems. Scoop out the gills with a spoon and discard. Coat the mushrooms with rapeseed oil. Top each mushroom evenly with the shredded Mozzarella cheese, followed by the minced walnuts. 3. Arrange the mushrooms in the air fryer and roast for 10 minutes until golden brown. 4. Transfer the mushrooms to a plate and sprinkle the parsley on top for garnish before serving.

Baked Jalapeño and Cheese Cauliflower Mash

Prep time: 10 minutes | Cook time: 15 minutes | Serves 6

1 (340 g) steamer bag cauliflower florets, cooked according to package instructions	120 g shredded sharp Cheddar cheese
2 tablespoons salted butter, softened	20 g pickled jalapeños
	½ teaspoon salt
60 g cream cheese, softened	¼ teaspoon ground black pepper

1. Place cooked cauliflower into a food processor with remaining ingredients. Pulse twenty times until cauliflower is smooth and all ingredients are combined. 2. Spoon mash into an ungreased round nonstick baking dish. Place dish into air fryer basket. Adjust the temperature to 192ºC and bake for 15 minutes. The top will be golden brown when done. Serve warm.

Cauliflower Rice Balls

Prep time: 10 minutes | Cook time: 8 minutes | Serves 4

1 (280 g) steamer bag cauliflower rice, cooked according to package instructions	1 large egg
	60 g plain pork scratchings, finely crushed
110 g shredded Mozzarella cheese	¼ teaspoon salt
	½ teaspoon Italian seasoning

1. Place cauliflower into a large bowl and mix with Mozzarella. 2. Whisk egg in a separate medium bowl. Place pork scratchings into another large bowl with salt and Italian seasoning. 3. Separate cauliflower mixture into four equal sections and form each into a ball. Carefully dip a ball into whisked egg, then roll in pork scratchings. Repeat with remaining balls. 4. Place cauliflower balls into ungreased air fryer basket. Adjust the temperature to 200ºC and air fry for 8 minutes. Rice balls will be golden when done. 5. Use a spatula to carefully move cauliflower balls to a large dish for serving. Serve warm.

Dinner Rolls

Prep time: 10 minutes | Cook time: 12 minutes | Serves 6

225 g shredded Mozzarella cheese	almond flour
30 g full-fat cream cheese	40 g ground flaxseed
95 g blanched finely ground	½ teaspoon baking powder
	1 large egg

1. Place Mozzarella, cream cheese, and almond flour in a large microwave-safe bowl. Microwave for 1 minute. Mix until smooth. 2. Add flaxseed, baking powder, and egg until fully combined and smooth. Microwave an additional 15 seconds if it becomes too firm. 3. Separate the dough into six pieces and roll into balls. Place the balls into the air fryer basket. 4. Adjust the temperature to 160°C and air fry for 12 minutes. 5. Allow rolls to cool completely before serving.

"Faux-Tato" Hash

Prep time: 10 minutes | Cook time: 12 minutes | Serves 4

450 g radishes, ends removed, quartered	2 tablespoons salted butter, melted
¼ medium yellow onion, peeled and diced	½ teaspoon garlic powder
½ medium green pepper, seeded and chopped	¼ teaspoon ground black pepper

1. In a large bowl, combine radishes, onion, and bell pepper. Toss with butter. 2. Sprinkle garlic powder and black pepper over mixture in bowl, then spoon into ungreased air fryer basket. 3. Adjust the temperature to 160°C and air fry for 12 minutes. Shake basket halfway through cooking. Radishes will be tender when done. Serve warm.

Super Cheesy Gold Aubergine

Prep time: 15 minutes | Cook time: 30 minutes | Serves 4

1 medium aubergine, peeled and cut into ½-inch-thick rounds	cheese
1 teaspoon salt, plus more for seasoning	Freshly ground black pepper, to taste
60 g plain flour	Cooking oil spray
2 eggs	180 g marinara sauce
90 g Italian bread crumbs	45 g shredded Parmesan cheese, divided
2 tablespoons grated Parmesan	110 g shredded Mozzarella cheese, divided

1. Blot the aubergine with paper towels to dry completely. You can also sprinkle with 1 teaspoon of salt to sweat out the moisture; if you do this, rinse the aubergine slices and blot dry again. 2. Place the flour in a shallow bowl. 3. In another shallow bowl, beat the eggs. 4. In a third shallow bowl, stir together the bread crumbs and grated Parmesan cheese and season with salt and pepper. 5. Dip each aubergine round in the flour, in the eggs, and into the bread crumbs to coat. 6. Insert the crisper plate into the basket and the basket into the unit. Preheat the unit by selecting AIR FRY, setting the temperature to 200°C, and setting the time to 3 minutes. Select START/STOP to begin. 7. Once the unit is preheated, spray the crisper plate and the basket with cooking oil. Working in batches, place the aubergine rounds into the basket. Do not stack them. Spray the aubergine with the cooking oil. 8. Select AIR FRY, set the temperature to 200°C, and set the time to 10 minutes. Select START/STOP to begin. 9. After 7 minutes, open the unit and top each round with 1 teaspoon of marinara sauce and ½ tablespoon each of shredded Parmesan and Mozzarella cheese. Resume cooking for 2 to 3 minutes until the cheese melts. 10. Repeat steps 5, 6, 7, 8, and 9 with the remaining aubergine. 11. When the cooking is complete, serve immediately.

Cauliflower with Lime Juice

Prep time: 10 minutes | Cook time: 7 minutes | Serves 4

215 g chopped cauliflower florets	½ teaspoon garlic powder
2 tablespoons coconut oil, melted	1 medium lime
2 teaspoons chili powder	2 tablespoons chopped coriander

1. In a large bowl, toss cauliflower with coconut oil. Sprinkle with chili powder and garlic powder. Place seasoned cauliflower into the air fryer basket. 2. Adjust the temperature to 180°C and set the timer for 7 minutes. 3. Cauliflower will be tender and begin to turn golden at the edges. Place into a serving bowl. 4. Cut the lime into quarters and squeeze juice over cauliflower. Garnish with coriander.

Mushrooms with Goat Cheese

Prep time: 10 minutes | Cook time: 10 minutes | Serves 4

3 tablespoons vegetable oil	½ teaspoon black pepper
450 g mixed mushrooms, trimmed and sliced	110 g goat cheese, diced
1 clove garlic, minced	2 teaspoons chopped fresh thyme leaves (optional)
¼ teaspoon dried thyme	

1. In a baking pan, combine the oil, mushrooms, garlic, dried thyme, and pepper. Stir in the goat cheese. Place the pan in the air fryer basket. Set the air fryer to 200°C for 10 minutes, stirring halfway through the cooking time. 2. Sprinkle with fresh thyme, if desired.

Crispy Lemon Artichoke Hearts

Prep time: 10 minutes | Cook time: 15 minutes | Serves 2

1 (425 g) can artichoke hearts in water, drained	30 g whole wheat bread crumbs
1 egg	¼ teaspoon salt
1 tablespoon water	¼ teaspoon paprika
	½ lemon

1. Preheat the air fryer to 192°C. 2. In a medium shallow bowl, beat together the egg and water until frothy. 3. In a separate medium shallow bowl, mix together the bread crumbs, salt, and paprika. 4. Dip each artichoke heart into the egg mixture, then into the bread crumb mixture, coating the outside with the crumbs. Place the artichokes hearts in a single layer of the air fryer basket. 5. Fry the artichoke hearts for 15 minutes. 6. Remove the artichokes from the air fryer, and squeeze fresh lemon juice over the top before serving.

Garlic Roasted Broccoli

Prep time: 8 minutes | Cook time: 10 to 14 minutes | Serves 6

1 head broccoli, cut into bite-size florets	Sea salt and freshly ground black pepper, to taste
1 tablespoon avocado oil	1 tablespoon freshly squeezed lemon juice
2 teaspoons minced garlic	½ teaspoon lemon zest
⅛ teaspoon red pepper flakes	

1. In a large bowl, toss together the broccoli, avocado oil, garlic, red pepper flakes, salt, and pepper. 2. Set the air fryer to 192°C. Arrange the broccoli in a single layer in the air fryer basket, working in batches if necessary. Roast for 10 to 14 minutes, until the broccoli is lightly charred. 3. Place the florets in a medium bowl and toss with the lemon juice and lemon zest. Serve.

Parmesan Herb Focaccia Bread

Prep time: 10 minutes | Cook time: 10 minutes | Serves 6

225 g shredded Mozzarella cheese	½ teaspoon bicarbonate of soda
30 g) full-fat cream cheese	2 large eggs
95 g blanched finely ground almond flour	½ teaspoon garlic powder
40 g ground golden flaxseed	¼ teaspoon dried basil
20 g grated Parmesan cheese	¼ teaspoon dried rosemary
	2 tablespoons salted butter, melted and divided

1. Place Mozzarella, cream cheese, and almond flour into a large microwave-safe bowl and microwave for 1 minute. Add the flaxseed, Parmesan, and bicarbonate of soda and stir until smooth ball forms. If the mixture cools too much, it will be hard to mix. Return to microwave for 10 to 15 seconds to rewarm if necessary.

2. Stir in eggs. You may need to use your hands to get them fully incorporated. Just keep stirring and they will absorb into the dough. 3. Sprinkle dough with garlic powder, basil, and rosemary and knead into dough. Grease a baking pan with 1 tablespoon melted butter. Press the dough evenly into the pan. Place pan into the air fryer basket. 4. Adjust the temperature to 200°C and bake for 10 minutes. 5. At 7 minutes, cover with foil if bread begins to get too dark. 6. Remove and let cool at least 30 minutes. Drizzle with remaining butter and serve.

Burger Bun for One

Prep time: 2 minutes | Cook time: 5 minutes | Serves 1

2 tablespoons salted butter, melted	¼ teaspoon baking powder
25 g blanched finely ground almond flour	⅛ teaspoon apple cider vinegar
	1 large egg, whisked

1. Pour butter into an ungreased ramekin. Add flour, baking powder, and vinegar to ramekin and stir until combined. Add egg and stir until batter is mostly smooth. 2. Place ramekin into air fryer basket. Adjust the temperature to 180°C and bake for 5 minutes. When done, the centre will be firm and the top slightly browned. Let cool, about 5 minutes, then remove from ramekin and slice in half. Serve.

Lemony Broccoli

Prep time: 10 minutes | Cook time: 9 to 14 minutes per batch | Serves 4

1 large head broccoli, rinsed and patted dry	1 tablespoon freshly squeezed lemon juice
2 teaspoons extra-virgin olive oil	Olive oil spray

1. Cut off the broccoli florets and separate them. You can use the stems, too; peel the stems and cut them into 1-inch chunks. 2. Insert the crisper plate into the basket and the basket into the unit. Preheat the unit by selecting AIR ROAST, setting the temperature to 200°C, and setting the time to 3 minutes. Select START/STOP to begin. 3. In a large bowl, toss together the broccoli, olive oil, and lemon juice until coated. 4. Once the unit is preheated, spray the crisper plate with olive oil. Working in batches, place half the broccoli into the basket. 5. Select AIR ROAST, set the temperature to 200°C, and set the time to 14 minutes. Select START/STOP to begin. 6. After 5 minutes, remove the basket and shake the broccoli. Reinsert the basket to resume cooking. Check the broccoli after 5 minutes. If it is crisp-tender and slightly brown around the edges, it is done. If not, resume cooking. 7. When the cooking is complete, transfer the broccoli to a serving bowl. Repeat steps 5 and 6 with the remaining broccoli. Serve immediately.

Maple-Roasted Tomatoes

Prep time: 15 minutes | Cook time: 20 minutes | Serves 2

280 g cherry tomatoes, halved	2 sprigs fresh thyme, stems
coarse sea salt, to taste	removed
2 tablespoons maple syrup	1 garlic clove, minced
1 tablespoon vegetable oil	Freshly ground black pepper

1. Place the tomatoes in a colander and sprinkle liberally with salt. Let stand for 10 minutes to drain. 2. Transfer the tomatoes cut-side up to a cake pan, then drizzle with the maple syrup, followed by the oil. Sprinkle with the thyme leaves and garlic and season with pepper. Place the pan in the air fryer and roast at 160ºC until the tomatoes are soft, collapsed, and lightly caramelized on top, about 20 minutes. 3. Serve straight from the pan or transfer the tomatoes to a plate and drizzle with the juices from the pan to serve.

Curried Fruit

Prep time: 10 minutes | Cook time: 20 minutes | Serves 6 to 8

210 g cubed fresh pineapple	425 g can dark, sweet, pitted
200 g cubed fresh pear (firm,	cherries with juice
not overly ripe)	2 tablespoons brown sugar
230 g frozen peaches, thawed	1 teaspoon curry powder

1. Combine all ingredients in large bowl. Stir gently to mix in the sugar and curry. 2. Pour into a baking pan and bake at 180ºC for 10 minutes. 3. Stir fruit and cook 10 more minutes. 4. Serve hot.

Sweet-and-Sour Brussels Sprouts

Prep time: 10 minutes | Cook time: 20 minutes | Serves 2

70 g Thai sweet chili sauce	2 small shallots, cut into
2 tablespoons black vinegar or	¼-inch-thick slices
balsamic vinegar	coarse sea salt and freshly
½ teaspoon hot sauce, such as	ground black pepper, to taste
Tabasco	2 teaspoons lightly packed fresh
230 g Brussels sprouts, trimmed	coriander leaves
(large sprouts halved)	

1. In a large bowl, whisk together the chili sauce, vinegar, and hot sauce. Add the Brussels sprouts and shallots, season with salt and pepper, and toss to combine. Scrape the Brussels sprouts and sauce into a cake pan. 2. Place the pan in the air fryer and roast at 192ºC, stirring every 5 minutes, until the Brussels sprouts are tender and the sauce is reduced to a sticky glaze, about 20 minutes. 3. Remove the pan from the air fryer and transfer the Brussels sprouts to plates. Sprinkle with the coriander and serve warm.

Lemon-Thyme Asparagus

Prep time: 5 minutes | Cook time: 4 to 8 minutes | Serves 4

450 g asparagus, woody ends	Sea salt and freshly ground
trimmed off	black pepper, to taste
1 tablespoon avocado oil	60 g goat cheese, crumbled
½ teaspoon dried thyme or	Zest and juice of 1 lemon
½ tablespoon chopped fresh	Flaky sea salt, for serving
thyme	(optional)

1. In a medium bowl, toss together the asparagus, avocado oil, and thyme, and season with sea salt and pepper. 2. Place the asparagus in the air fryer basket in a single layer. Set the air fryer to 200ºC and air fry for 4 to 8 minutes, to your desired doneness. 3. Transfer to a serving platter. Top with the goat cheese, lemon zest, and lemon juice. If desired, season with a pinch of flaky salt.

Roasted Potatoes and Asparagus

Prep time: 5 minutes | Cook time: 23 minutes | Serves 4

4 medium potatoes	1 tablespoon wholegrain
1 bunch asparagus	mustard
75 g cottage cheese	Salt and pepper, to taste
80 g low-fat crème fraiche	Cooking spray

1. Preheat the air fryer to 200ºC. Spritz the air fryer basket with cooking spray. 2. Place the potatoes in the basket. Air fry the potatoes for 20 minutes. 3. Boil the asparagus in salted water for 3 minutes. 4. Remove the potatoes and mash them with rest of ingredients. Sprinkle with salt and pepper. 5. Serve immediately.

Air Fried Potatoes with Olives

Prep time: 15 minutes | Cook time: 40 minutes | Serves 1

1 medium Maris Piper potatoes,	Dollop of butter
scrubbed and peeled	Dollop of cream cheese
1 teaspoon olive oil	1 tablespoon Kalamata olives
¼ teaspoon onion powder	1 tablespoon chopped chives
⅛ teaspoon salt	

1. Preheat the air fryer to 200ºC. 2. In a bowl, coat the potatoes with the onion powder, salt, olive oil, and butter. 3. Transfer to the air fryer and air fry for 40 minutes, turning the potatoes over at the halfway point. 4. Take care when removing the potatoes from the air fryer and serve with the cream cheese, Kalamata olives and chives on top.

Mashed Sweet Potato Tots

Prep time: 10 minutes | Cook time: 12 to 13 minutes per batch | Makes 18 to 24 tots

210 g cooked mashed sweet potatoes	2 tablespoons chopped pecans
1 egg white, beaten	1½ teaspoons honey
⅛ teaspoon ground cinnamon	Salt, to taste
1 dash nutmeg	50 g panko bread crumbs
	Oil for misting or cooking spray

1. Preheat the air fryer to 200°C. 2. In a large bowl, mix together the potatoes, egg white, cinnamon, nutmeg, pecans, honey, and salt to taste. 3. Place panko crumbs on a sheet of wax paper. 4. For each tot, use about 2 teaspoons of sweet potato mixture. To shape, drop the measure of potato mixture onto panko crumbs and push crumbs up and around potatoes to coat edges. Then turn tot over to coat other side with crumbs. 5. Mist tots with oil or cooking spray and place in air fryer basket in single layer. 6. Air fry at 200°C for 12 to 13 minutes, until browned and crispy. 7. Repeat steps 5 and 6 to cook remaining tots.

Citrus-Roasted Broccoli Florets

Prep time: 5 minutes | Cook time: 12 minutes | Serves 6

285 g broccoli florets (approximately 1 large head)	130 ml orange juice
2 tablespoons olive oil	1 tablespoon raw honey
½ teaspoon salt	Orange wedges, for serving (optional)

1. Preheat the air fryer to 180°C. 2. In a large bowl, combine the broccoli, olive oil, salt, orange juice, and honey. Toss the broccoli in the liquid until well coated. 3. Pour the broccoli mixture into the air fryer basket and roast for 6 minutes. Stir and roast for 6 minutes more. 4. Serve alone or with orange wedges for additional citrus flavour, if desired.

Golden Garlicky Mushrooms

Prep time: 10 minutes | Cook time: 10 minutes | Serves 4

6 small mushrooms	1 teaspoon parsley
1 tablespoon bread crumbs	1 teaspoon garlic purée
1 tablespoon olive oil	Salt and ground black pepper, to taste
30 g onion, peeled and diced	

1. Preheat the air fryer to 180°C. 2. Combine the bread crumbs, oil, onion, parsley, salt, pepper and garlic in a bowl. Cut out the mushrooms' stalks and stuff each cap with the crumb mixture. 3. Air fry in the air fryer for 10 minutes. 4. Serve hot.

Bacon Potatoes and Green Beans

Prep time: 10 minutes | Cook time: 25 minutes | Serves 4

Oil, for spraying	280 g fresh green beans
900 g medium Maris Piper potatoes, quartered	1 teaspoon salt
100 g bacon bits	½ teaspoon freshly ground black pepper

1. Line the air fryer basket with parchment and spray lightly with oil. 2. Place the potatoes in the prepared basket. Top with the bacon bits and green beans. Sprinkle with the salt and black pepper and spray liberally with oil. 3. Air fry at 180°C for 25 minutes, stirring after 12 minutes and spraying with oil, until the potatoes are easily pierced with a fork.

Buttery Mushrooms

Prep time: 10 minutes | Cook time: 10 minutes | Serves 4

230 g shitake mushrooms, halved	¼ teaspoon salt
2 tablespoons salted butter, melted	¼ teaspoon ground black pepper

1. In a medium bowl, toss mushrooms with butter, then sprinkle with salt and pepper. Place into ungreased air fryer basket. Adjust the temperature to 200°C and air fry for 10 minutes, shaking the basket halfway through cooking. Mushrooms will be tender when done. Serve warm.

Fig, Chickpea, and Rocket Salad

Prep time: 15 minutes | Cook time: 20 minutes | Serves 4

8 fresh figs, halved	2 tablespoons extra-virgin olive oil, plus more for greasing
250 g cooked chickpeas	
1 teaspoon crushed roasted cumin seeds	Salt and ground black pepper, to taste
4 tablespoons balsamic vinegar	40 g rocket, washed and dried

1. Preheat the air fryer to 192°C. 2. Cover the air fryer basket with aluminum foil and grease lightly with oil. Put the figs in the air fryer basket and air fry for 10 minutes. 3. In a bowl, combine the chickpeas and cumin seeds. 4. Remove the air fried figs from the air fryer and replace with the chickpeas. Air fry for 10 minutes. Leave to cool. 5. In the meantime, prepare the dressing. Mix the balsamic vinegar, olive oil, salt and pepper. 6. In a salad bowl, combine the rocket with the cooled figs and chickpeas. 7. Toss with the sauce and serve.

Garlic Herb Radishes

Prep time: 10 minutes | Cook time: 10 minutes | Serves 4

450 g radishes
2 tablespoons unsalted butter, melted
½ teaspoon garlic powder

½ teaspoon dried parsley
¼ teaspoon dried oregano
¼ teaspoon ground black pepper

1. Remove roots from radishes and cut into quarters. 2. In a small bowl, add butter and seasonings. Toss the radishes in the herb butter and place into the air fryer basket. 3. Adjust the temperature to 180°C and set the timer for 10 minutes. 4. Halfway through the cooking time, toss the radishes in the air fryer basket. Continue cooking until edges begin to turn brown. 5. Serve warm.

Broccoli with Sesame Dressing

Prep time: 5 minutes | Cook time: 10 minutes | Serves 4

425 g broccoli florets, cut into bite-size pieces
1 tablespoon olive oil
¼ teaspoon salt
2 tablespoons sesame seeds
2 tablespoons rice vinegar

2 tablespoons coconut aminos
2 tablespoons sesame oil
½ teaspoon xylitol
¼ teaspoon red pepper flakes (optional)

1. Preheat the air fryer to 200°C. 2. In a large bowl, toss the broccoli with the olive oil and salt until thoroughly coated. 3. Transfer the broccoli to the air fryer basket. Pausing halfway through the cooking time to shake the basket, air fry for 10 minutes until the stems are tender and the edges are beginning to crisp. 4. Meanwhile, in the same large bowl, whisk together the sesame seeds, vinegar, coconut aminos, sesame oil, xylitol, and red pepper flakes (if using). 5. Transfer the broccoli to the bowl and toss until thoroughly coated with the seasonings. Serve warm or at room temperature.

Roasted Salsa

Prep time: 15 minutes | Cook time: 30 minutes | Makes 500 g

2 large San Marzano tomatoes, cored and cut into large chunks
½ medium white onion, peeled and large-diced
½ medium jalapeño, seeded and large-diced

2 cloves garlic, peeled and diced
½ teaspoon salt
1 tablespoon coconut oil
65 ml fresh lime juice

1. Place tomatoes, onion, and jalapeño into an ungreased round nonstick baking dish. Add garlic, then sprinkle with salt and drizzle with coconut oil. 2. Place dish into air fryer basket. Adjust the temperature to 150°C and bake for 30 minutes. Vegetables will be dark brown around the edges and tender when done. 3. Pour mixture into a food processor or blender. Add lime juice. Process on low speed 30 seconds until only a few chunks remain. 4. Transfer salsa to a sealable container and refrigerate at least 1 hour. Serve chilled.

Five-Spice Roasted Sweet Potatoes

Prep time: 10 minutes | Cook time: 12 minutes | Serves 4

½ teaspoon ground cinnamon
¼ teaspoon ground cumin
¼ teaspoon paprika
1 teaspoon chili powder
⅛ teaspoon turmeric
½ teaspoon salt (optional)

Freshly ground black pepper, to taste
2 large sweet potatoes, peeled and cut into ¾-inch cubes
1 tablespoon olive oil

1. In a large bowl, mix together cinnamon, cumin, paprika, chili powder, turmeric, salt, and pepper to taste. 2. Add potatoes and stir well. 3. Drizzle the seasoned potatoes with the olive oil and stir until evenly coated. 4. Place seasoned potatoes in a baking pan or an ovenproof dish that fits inside your air fryer basket. 5. Cook for 6 minutes at 200°C, stop, and stir well. 6. Cook for an additional 6 minutes.

Easy Greek Briami (Ratatouille)

Prep time: 15 minutes | Cook time: 40 minutes | Serves 6

2 Maris Piper potatoes, cubed
100 g plum tomatoes, cubed
1 aubergine, cubed
1 courgette, cubed
1 red onion, chopped
1 red pepper, chopped
2 garlic cloves, minced
1 teaspoon dried mint
1 teaspoon dried parsley

1 teaspoon dried oregano
½ teaspoon salt
½ teaspoon black pepper
¼ teaspoon red pepper flakes
80 ml olive oil
1 (230 g) can tomato paste
65 ml vegetable stock
65 ml water

1. Preheat the air fryer to 160°C. 2. In a large bowl, combine the potatoes, tomatoes, aubergine, courgette onion, bell pepper, garlic, mint, parsley, oregano, salt, black pepper, and red pepper flakes. 3. In a small bowl, mix together the olive oil, tomato paste, stock, and water. 4. Pour the oil-and-tomato-paste mixture over the vegetables and toss until everything is coated. 5. Pour the coated vegetables into the air fryer basket in an even layer and roast for 20 minutes. After 20 minutes, stir well and spread out again. Roast for an additional 10 minutes, then repeat the process and cook for another 10 minutes.

Shishito Pepper Roast

Prep time: 4 minutes | Cook time: 9 minutes | Serves 4

Cooking oil spray (sunflower, safflower, or refined coconut)

450 g shishito, Anaheim, or bell peppers, rinsed

1 tablespoon soy sauce

2 teaspoons freshly squeezed lime juice

2 large garlic cloves, pressed

1. Insert the crisper plate into the basket and the basket into the unit. Preheat the unit by selecting AIR ROAST, setting the temperature to 200ºC, and setting the time to 3 minutes. Select START/STOP to begin. 2. Once the unit is preheated, spray the crisper plate and the basket with cooking oil. Place the peppers into the basket and spray them with oil. 3. Select AIR ROAST, set the temperature to 200ºC, and set the time to 9 minutes. Select START/STOP to begin. 4. After 3 minutes, remove the basket and shake the peppers. Spray the peppers with more oil. Reinsert the basket to resume cooking. Repeat this step again after 3 minutes. 5. While the peppers roast, in a medium bowl, whisk the soy sauce, lime juice, and garlic until combined. Set aside. 6. When the cooking is complete, several of the peppers should have lots of nice browned spots on them. If using Anaheim or bell peppers, cut a slit in the side of each pepper and remove the seeds, which can be bitter. 7. Place the roasted peppers in the bowl with the sauce. Toss to coat the peppers evenly and serve.

Flatbread

Prep time: 5 minutes | Cook time: 7 minutes | Serves 2

225 g shredded Mozzarella cheese

25 g blanched finely ground

almond flour

30 g full-fat cream cheese, softened

1. In a large microwave-safe bowl, melt Mozzarella in the microwave for 30 seconds. Stir in almond flour until smooth and then add cream cheese. Continue mixing until dough forms, gently kneading it with wet hands if necessary. 2. Divide the dough into two pieces and roll out to ¼-inch thickness between two pieces of parchment. Cut another piece of parchment to fit your air fryer basket. 3. Place a piece of flatbread onto your parchment and into the air fryer, working in two batches if needed. 4. Adjust the temperature to 160ºC and air fry for 7 minutes. 5. Halfway through the cooking time flip the flatbread. Serve warm.

Garlic Courgette and Red Peppers

Prep time: 5 minutes | Cook time: 15 minutes | Serves 6

2 medium courgette, cubed

1 red pepper, diced

2 garlic cloves, sliced

2 tablespoons olive oil

½ teaspoon salt

1. Preheat the air fryer to 193ºC. 2. In a large bowl, mix together the courgette, bell pepper, and garlic with the olive oil and salt. 3. Pour the mixture into the air fryer basket, and roast for 7 minutes. Shake or stir, then roast for 7 to 8 minutes more.

Gold Artichoke Hearts

Prep time: 15 minutes | Cook time: 8 minutes | Serves 4

12 whole artichoke hearts packed in water, drained

60 g plain flour

1 egg

40 g panko bread crumbs

1 teaspoon Italian seasoning

Cooking oil spray

1. Squeeze any excess water from the artichoke hearts and place them on paper towels to dry. 2. Place the flour in a small bowl. 3. In another small bowl, beat the egg. 4. In a third small bowl, stir together the panko and Italian seasoning. 5. Dip the artichoke hearts in the flour, in the egg, and into the panko mixture until coated. 6. Insert the crisper plate into the basket and the basket into the unit. Preheat the unit by selecting AIR FRY, setting the temperature to 192ºC, and setting the time to 3 minutes. Select START/STOP to begin. 7. Once the unit is preheated, spray the crisper plate and the basket with cooking oil. Place the breaded artichoke hearts into the basket, stacking them if needed. 8. Select AIR FRY, set the temperature to 192ºC, and set the time to 8 minutes. Select START/STOP to begin. 9. After 4 minutes, use tongs to flip the artichoke hearts. I recommend flipping instead of shaking because the hearts are small, and this will help keep the breading intact. Re-insert the basket to resume cooking. 10. When the cooking is complete, the artichoke hearts should be deep golden brown and crisp. Cool for 5 minutes before serving.

Chapter 8 Desserts

Cream-Filled Sandwich Cookies

Prep time: 8 minutes | Cook time: 8 minutes | Makes 8 cookies

Coconut, or avocado oil, for spraying
1 tube croissant dough
60 ml milk
8 cream-filled sandwich biscuits
1 tablespoon icing sugar

1. Line the air fryer basket with baking paper, and spray lightly with oil. 2. Unroll the dough and cut it into 8 triangles. Lay out the triangles on a work surface. 3. Pour the milk into a shallow bowl. Quickly dip each cookie in the milk, then place in the center of a dough triangle. 4. Wrap the dough around the cookie, cutting off any excess and pinching the edges to seal. You may be able to combine the excess dough to cover additional cookies, if desired. 5. Place the wrapped cookies in the prepared basket, seam-side down, and spray lightly with oil. 6. Bake at 176°C for 4 minutes, flip, spray with oil, and cook for another 3 to 4 minutes, or until puffed and golden brown. 7. Dust with the icing sugar and serve.

Pineapple Galette

Prep time: 15 minutes | Cook time: 40 minutes | Serves 2

¼ medium-size pineapple, peeled, cored, and cut crosswise into ¼-inch-thick slices
2 tablespoons dark rum, or apple juice
1 teaspoon vanilla extract
½ teaspoon kosher, or coarse sea salt
Finely grated zest of ½ lime
1 store-bought sheet puff pastry, cut into an 8-inch round
3 tablespoons granulated sugar
2 tablespoons unsalted butter, cubed and chilled
Coconut ice cream, for serving

1. In a small bowl, combine the pineapple slices, rum, vanilla, salt, and lime zest and let stand for at least 10 minutes to allow the pineapple to soak in the rum. 2. Meanwhile, press the puff pastry round into the bottom and up the sides of a cake pan and use the tines of a fork to dock the bottom and sides. 3. Arrange the pineapple slices on the bottom of the pastry in a more or less single layer, then sprinkle with the sugar and dot with the butter. Drizzle with the leftover juices from the bowl. Place the pan in the air fryer and bake at 154°C until the pastry is puffed and golden brown and the pineapple is lightly caramelized on top, about 40 minutes. 4. Transfer the pan to a wire rack to cool for 15 minutes. Unmold the galette from the pan and serve warm with coconut ice cream.

Oatmeal Raisin Bars

Prep time: 15 minutes | Cook time: 15 minutes | Serves 8

40 g plain flour
¼ teaspoon kosher, or coarse sea salt
¼ teaspoon baking powder
¼ teaspoon ground cinnamon
50 g light brown sugar, lightly packed
50 g granulated sugar
120 ml canola, or rapeseed oil
1 large egg
1 teaspoon vanilla extract
110 g quick-cooking oats
60 g raisins

1. Preheat the air fryer to 184°C. 2. In a large bowl, combine the plain flour, kosher salt, baking powder, ground cinnamon, light brown sugar, granulated sugar, canola oil, egg, vanilla extract, quick-cooking oats, and raisins. 3. Spray a baking pan with nonstick cooking spray, then pour the oat mixture into the pan and press down to evenly distribute. Place the pan in the air fryer and bake for 15 minutes or until golden brown. 4. Remove from the air fryer and allow to cool in the pan on a wire rack for 20 minutes before slicing and serving.

Brown Sugar Banana Bread

Prep time: 20 minutes | Cook time: 22 to 24 minutes | Serves 4

195 g packed light brown sugar
1 large egg, beaten
2 tablespoons unsalted butter, melted
120 ml milk, whole or semi-skimmed
250 g plain flour
1½ teaspoons baking powder
1 teaspoon ground cinnamon
½ teaspoon salt
1 banana, mashed
1 to 2 tablespoons coconut, or avocado oil oil
30 g icing sugar (optional)

1. In a large bowl, stir together the brown sugar, egg, melted butter, and milk. 2. In a medium bowl, whisk the flour, baking powder, cinnamon, and salt until blended. Add the flour mixture to the sugar mixture and stir just to blend. 3. Add the mashed banana and stir to combine. 4. Preheat the air fryer to 176°C. Spritz 2 mini loaf pans with oil. 5. Evenly divide the batter between the prepared pans and place them in the air fryer basket. 6. Cook for 22 to 24 minutes, or until a knife inserted into the middle of the loaves comes out clean. 7. Dust the warm loaves with icing sugar (if using).

Grilled Pineapple Dessert

Prep time: 5 minutes | Cook time: 12 minutes | Serves 4

Coconut, or avocado oil for misting, or cooking spray

4 ½-inch-thick slices fresh pineapple, core removed

1 tablespoon honey

¼ teaspoon brandy, or apple

juice

2 tablespoons slivered almonds, toasted

Vanilla frozen yogurt, coconut sorbet, or ice cream

1. Spray both sides of pineapple slices with oil or cooking spray. Place into air fryer basket. 2. Air fry at 200°C for 6 minutes. Turn slices over and cook for an additional 6 minutes. 3. Mix together the honey and brandy. 4. Remove cooked pineapple slices from air fryer, sprinkle with toasted almonds, and drizzle with honey mixture. 5. Serve with a scoop of frozen yogurt or sorbet on the side.

Cinnamon-Sugar Almonds

Prep time: 5 minutes | Cook time: 8 minutes | Serves 4

150 g whole almonds

2 tablespoons salted butter, melted

1 tablespoon granulated sugar

½ teaspoon ground cinnamon

1. In a medium bowl, combine the almonds, butter, sugar, and cinnamon. Mix well to ensure all the almonds are coated with the spiced butter. 2. Transfer the almonds to the air fryer basket and shake so they are in a single layer. Set the air fryer to 148°C, and cook for 8 minutes, stirring the almonds halfway through the cooking time. 3. Let cool completely before serving.

Simple Apple Turnovers

Prep time: 10 minutes | Cook time: 10 minutes | Serves 4

1 apple, peeled, quartered, and thinly sliced

½ teaspoons pumpkin pie spice

Juice of ½ lemon

1 tablespoon granulated sugar

Pinch of kosher, or coarse sea salt

6 sheets filo pastry

1. Preheat the air fryer to 164°C. 2. In a medium bowl, combine the apple, pumpkin pie spice, lemon juice, granulated sugar, and kosher salt. 3. Cut the filo pastry sheets into 4 equal pieces and place individual tablespoons of apple filling in the center of each piece, then fold in both sides and roll from front to back. 4. Spray the air fryer basket with nonstick cooking spray, then place the turnovers in the basket and bake for 10 minutes or until golden brown. 5. Remove the turnovers from the air fryer and allow to cool on a wire rack for 10 minutes before serving.

Molten Chocolate Almond Cakes

Prep time: 5 minutes | Cook time: 13 minutes | Serves 3

Butter and flour for the ramekins

110 g bittersweet chocolate, chopped

110 gunsalted butter

2 eggs

2 egg yolks

50 g granulated sugar

½ teaspoon pure vanilla extract,

or almond extract

1 tablespoon plain flour

3 tablespoons ground almonds

8 to 12 semisweet chocolate discs (or 4 chunks of chocolate)

Cocoa powder or icing sugar, for dusting

Toasted almonds, coarsely chopped

1. Butter and flour three (170 g) ramekins. (Butter the ramekins and then coat the butter with flour by shaking it around in the ramekin and dumping out any excess.) 2. Melt the chocolate and butter together, either in the microwave or in a double boiler. In a separate bowl, beat the eggs, egg yolks and sugar together until light and smooth. Add the vanilla extract. Whisk the chocolate mixture into the egg mixture. Stir in the flour and ground almonds. 3. Preheat the air fryer to 164°C. 4. Transfer the batter carefully to the buttered ramekins, filling halfway. Place two or three chocolate discs in the center of the batter and then fill the ramekins to ½-inch below the top with the remaining batter. Place the ramekins into the air fryer basket and air fry for 13 minutes. The sides of the cake should be set, but the centers should be slightly soft. Remove the ramekins from the air fryer and let the cakes sit for 5 minutes. (If you'd like the cake a little less molten, air fry for 14 minutes and let the cakes sit for 4 minutes.) 5. Run a butter knife around the edge of the ramekins and invert the cakes onto a plate. Lift the ramekin off the plate slowly and carefully so that the cake doesn't break. Dust with cocoa powder or icing sugar and serve with a scoop of ice cream and some coarsely chopped toasted almonds.

Apple Wedges with Apricots

Prep time: 5 minutes | Cook time: 15 to 18 minutes | Serves 4

4 large apples, peeled and sliced into 8 wedges

2 tablespoons light olive oil

95 g dried apricots, chopped

1 to 2 tablespoons granulated sugar

½ teaspoon ground cinnamon

1. Preheat the air fryer to 180°C. 2. Toss the apple wedges with the olive oil in a mixing bowl until well coated. 3. Place the apple wedges in the air fryer basket and air fry for 12 to 15 minutes. 4. Sprinkle with the dried apricots and air fry for another 3 minutes. 5. Meanwhile, thoroughly combine the sugar and cinnamon in a small bowl. 6. Remove the apple wedges from the basket to a plate. Serve sprinkled with the sugar mixture.

Gluten-Free Spice Cookies

Prep time: 10 minutes | Cook time: 12 minutes | Serves 4

4 tablespoons unsalted butter, at room temperature	2 teaspoons ground ginger
2 tablespoons agave nectar	1 teaspoon ground cinnamon
1 large egg	½ teaspoon freshly grated nutmeg
2 tablespoons water	1 teaspoon baking soda
240 g almond flour	¼ teaspoon kosher, or coarse
100 g granulated sugar	sea salt

1. Line the bottom of the air fryer basket with baking paper cut to fit. 2. In a large bowl, using a hand mixer, beat together the butter, agave, egg, and water on medium speed until light and fluffy. 3. Add the almond flour, sugar, ginger, cinnamon, nutmeg, baking soda, and salt. Beat on low speed until well combined. 4. Roll the dough into 2-tablespoon balls and arrange them on the baking paper in the basket. (They don't really spread too much but try to leave a little room between them.) Set the air fryer to 164ºC, and cook for 12 minutes, or until the tops of cookies are lightly browned. 5. Transfer to a wire rack and let cool completely. Store in an airtight container for up to a week.

Mixed Berry Hand Pies

Prep time: 5 minutes | Cook time: 30 minutes | Serves 4

150 g granulated sugar	two equal portions
½ teaspoon ground cinnamon	1 teaspoon water
1 tablespoon cornflour	1 package refrigerated
150 g blueberries	shortcrust pastry (or your own
150 g blackberries	homemade pastry)
150 g raspberries, divided into	1 egg, beaten

1. Combine the sugar, cinnamon, and cornstarch in a small saucepan. Add the blueberries, blackberries, and ½ of the raspberries. Toss the berries gently to coat them evenly. Add the teaspoon of water to the saucepan and turn the stovetop on to medium-high heat, stirring occasionally. Once the berries break down, release their juice, and start to simmer (about 5 minutes), simmer for another couple of minutes and then transfer the mixture to a bowl, stir in the remaining ½ of the raspberries and let it cool. 2. Preheat the air fryer to 188ºC. 3. Cut the pie dough into four 5-inch circles and four 6-inch circles. 4. Spread the 6-inch circles on a flat surface. Divide the berry filling between all four circles. Brush the perimeter of the dough circles with a little water. Place the 5-inch circles on top of the filling and press the perimeter of the dough circles together to seal. Roll the edges of the bottom circle up over the top circle to make a crust around the filling. Press a fork around the crust to make decorative indentations and to seal the crust shut. Brush the pies with egg wash and sprinkle a little sugar on top. Poke a small hole in the center of each pie with a paring knife to vent the dough. 5. Air fry two pies at a time. Brush or spray the air fryer basket with oil and place the pies into the basket. Air fry for 9 minutes. Turn the pies over and air fry for another 6 minutes. Serve warm or at room temperature.

Double Chocolate Brownies

Prep time: 5 minutes | Cook time: 15 to 20 minutes | Serves 8

110 g almond flour	110 g unsalted butter, melted and cooled
50 g unsweetened cocoa powder	3 eggs
½ teaspoon baking powder	1 teaspoon vanilla extract
35 g powdered sweetener	2 tablespoons mini semisweet
¼ teaspoon salt	chocolate chips

1. Preheat the air fryer to 176ºC. Line a cake pan with baking paper and brush with oil. 2. In a large bowl, combine the almond flour, cocoa powder, baking powder, sweetener, and salt. Add the butter, eggs, and vanilla. Stir until thoroughly combined (the batter will be thick.) Spread the batter into the prepared pan and scatter the chocolate chips on top. 3. Air fry for 15 to 20 minutes until the edges are set (the center should still appear slightly undercooked.) Let cool completely before slicing. To store, cover and refrigerate the brownies for up to 3 days.

Courgette Nut Muffins

Prep time: 15 minutes | Cook time: 15 minutes | Serves 4

60 ml vegetable oil, plus more for greasing	¼ teaspoon baking soda
90 g plain flour	¼ teaspoon baking powder
¾ teaspoon ground cinnamon	2 large eggs
¼ teaspoon kosher, or coarse sea salt	100 g granulated sugar
	90 g grated courgette
	35 g chopped walnuts

1. Generously grease four ramekins or a baking pan with vegetable oil. 2. In a medium bowl, sift together the flour, cinnamon, salt, baking soda, and baking powder. 3. In a separate medium bowl, beat together the eggs, sugar, and vegetable oil. Add the dry ingredients to the wet ingredients. Add the courgette and nuts and stir gently until well combined. Transfer the batter to the prepared ramekins or baking pan. 4. Place the ramekins or pan in the air fryer basket. Set the air fryer to 164ºC, and cook for 15 minutes, or until a cake tester or toothpick inserted into the center comes out clean. If it doesn't, cook for 3 to 5 minutes more and test again. 5. Let cool in the ramekins or pan on a wire rack for 10 minutes. Carefully remove from the ramekins or pan and let cool completely on the rack before serving.

Brownies for Two

Prep time: 5 minutes | Cook time: 15 minutes | Serves 2

50 g blanched finely ground almond flour	½ teaspoon baking powder
3 tablespoons granulated sweetener	1 teaspoon vanilla extract
3 tablespoons unsweetened cocoa powder	2 large eggs, whisked
	2 tablespoons salted butter, melted

1. In a medium bowl, combine flour, sweetener, cocoa powder, and baking powder. 2. Add in vanilla, eggs, and butter, and stir until a thick batter forms. 3. Pour batter into two ramekins greased with cooking spray and place ramekins into air fryer basket. Adjust the temperature to 164°C and bake for 15 minutes. Centers will be firm when done. Let ramekins cool 5 minutes before serving.

Mixed Berries with Pecan Streusel Topping

Prep time: 5 minutes | Cook time: 17 minutes | Serves 3

75 g mixed berries	2 tablespoons chopped walnuts
Cooking spray	3 tablespoons granulated sweetener
Topping:	
1 egg, beaten	2 tablespoons cold salted butter, cut into pieces
3 tablespoons almonds, slivered	
3 tablespoons chopped pecans	½ teaspoon ground cinnamon

1. Preheat the air fryer to 172°C. Lightly spray a baking dish with cooking spray. 2. Make the topping: In a medium bowl, stir together the beaten egg, nuts, sweetener, butter, and cinnamon until well blended. 3. Put the mixed berries in the bottom of the baking dish and spread the topping over the top. 4. Bake in the preheated air fryer for 17 minutes, or until the fruit is bubbly and topping is golden brown. 5. Allow to cool for 5 to 10 minutes before serving.

Lemon Poppy Seed Macaroons

Prep time: 10 minutes | Cook time: 14 minutes | Makes 1 dozen

cookies

2 large egg whites, room temperature	1 teaspoon lemon extract
35 g powdered sweetener	¼ teaspoon fine sea salt
2 tablespoons grated lemon zest, plus more for garnish if desired	190 g desiccated unsweetened coconut
	Lemon Icing:
2 teaspoons poppy seeds	25 g sweetener
	1 tablespoon lemon juice

1. Preheat the air fryer to 164°C. Line a pie pan or a casserole dish that will fit inside your air fryer with baking paper. 2. Place the egg whites in a medium-sized bowl and use a hand mixer on high to beat the whites until stiff peaks form. Add the sweetener, lemon zest, poppy seeds, lemon extract, and salt. Mix on low until combined. Gently fold in the coconut with a rubber spatula. 3. Use a 1-inch cookie scoop to place the cookies on the baking paper, spacing them about ¼ inch apart. Place the pan in the air fryer and bake for 12 to 14 minutes, until the cookies are golden, and a toothpick inserted into the center comes out clean. 4. While the cookies bake, make the lemon icing: Place the sweetener in a small bowl. Add the lemon juice and stir well. If the icing is too thin, add a little more sweetener. If the icing is too thick, add a little more lemon juice. 5. Remove the cookies from the air fryer and allow to cool for about 10 minutes, then drizzle with the icing. Garnish with lemon zest, if desired. Store leftovers in an airtight container in the fridge for up to 5 days or in the freezer for up to a month.

Zucchini Bread

Prep time: 10 minutes | Cook time: 40 minutes | Serves 12

220 g coconut flour	1 teaspoon vanilla extract
2 teaspoons baking powder	3 eggs, beaten
150 g granulated sweetener	1 courgette, grated
120 ml coconut oil, melted	1 teaspoon ground cinnamon
1 teaspoon apple cider vinegar	

1. In the mixing bowl, mix coconut flour with baking powder, sweetener, coconut oil, apple cider vinegar, vanilla extract, eggs, courgette, and ground cinnamon. 2. Transfer the mixture into the air fryer basket and flatten it in the shape of the bread. 3. Cook the bread at 176°C for 40 minutes.

Protein Powder Doughnut Holes

Prep time: 25 minutes | Cook time: 6 minutes | Makes 12 holes

50 g blanched finely ground almond flour	½ teaspoon baking powder
	1 large egg
60 g low-carb vanilla protein powder	5 tablespoons unsalted butter, melted
100 g granulated sweetener	½ teaspoon vanilla extract

1. Mix all ingredients in a large bowl. Place into the freezer for 20 minutes. 2. Wet your hands with water and roll the dough into twelve balls. 3. Cut a piece of baking paper to fit your air fryer basket. Working in batches as necessary, place doughnut holes into the air fryer basket on top of baking paper. 4. Adjust the temperature to 192°C and air fry for 6 minutes. 5. Flip doughnut holes halfway through the cooking time. 6. Let cool completely before serving.

Cinnamon and Pecan Pie

Prep time: 10 minutes | Cook time: 25 minutes | Serves 4

1 pack shortcrust pastry	⅛ teaspoon nutmeg
½ teaspoons cinnamon	3 tablespoons melted butter,
¾ teaspoon vanilla extract	divided
2 eggs	2 tablespoons sugar
175 ml maple syrup	65 g chopped pecans

1. Preheat the air fryer to 188ºC. 2. In a small bowl, coat the pecans in 1 tablespoon of melted butter. 3. Transfer the pecans to the air fryer and air fry for about 10 minutes. 4. Put the pie dough in a greased pie pan, trim off the excess and add the pecans on top. 5. In a bowl, mix the rest of the ingredients. Pour this over the pecans. 6. Put the pan in the air fryer and bake for 25 minutes. 7. Serve immediately.

Breaded Bananas with Chocolate Topping

Prep time: 10 minutes | Cook time: 10 minutes | Serves 6

40 g cornflour	3 bananas, halved crosswise
25 g plain breadcrumbs	Cooking spray
1 large egg, beaten	Chocolate sauce, for serving

1. Preheat the air fryer to176ºC. 2. Place the cornflour, breadcrumbs, and egg in three separate bowls. 3. Roll the bananas in the cornstarch, then in the beaten egg, and finally in the breadcrumbs to coat well. 4. Spritz the air fryer basket with the cooking spray. 5. Arrange the banana halves in the basket and mist them with the cooking spray. Air fry for 5 minutes. Flip the bananas and continue to air fry for another 2 minutes. 6. Remove the bananas from the basket to a serving plate. Serve with the chocolate sauce drizzled over the top.

Pecan Brownies

Prep time: 10 minutes | Cook time: 20 minutes | Serves 6

50 g blanched finely ground almond flour	55 g unsalted butter, softened
55 g powdered sweetener	1 large egg
2 tablespoons unsweetened cocoa powder	35 g chopped pecans
	40 g low-carb, sugar-free chocolate chips
½ teaspoon baking powder	

1. In a large bowl, mix almond flour, sweetener, cocoa powder, and baking powder. Stir in butter and egg. 2. Fold in pecans and chocolate chips. Scoop mixture into a round baking pan. Place pan into the air fryer basket. 3. Adjust the temperature to 148ºC and bake for 20 minutes. 4. When fully cooked a toothpick inserted in center will come out clean. Allow 20 minutes to fully cool and firm up.

New York Cheesecake

Prep time: 1 hour | Cook time: 37 minutes | Serves 8

170 g almond flour	340 g granulated sweetener
85 g powdered sweetener	3 eggs, at room temperature
55 g unsalted butter, melted	1 tablespoon vanilla essence
565 g full-fat cream cheese	1 teaspoon grated lemon zest
120 ml heavy cream	

1. Coat the sides and bottom of a baking pan with a little flour. 2. In a mixing bowl, combine the almond flour and powdered sweetener. Add the melted butter and mix until your mixture looks like breadcrumbs. 3. Press the mixture into the bottom of the prepared pan to form an even layer. Bake at 164ºC for 7 minutes until golden brown. Allow it to cool completely on a wire rack. 4. Meanwhile, in a mixer fitted with the paddle attachment, prepare the filling by mixing the soft cheese, heavy cream, and granulated sweetener; beat until creamy and fluffy. 5. Crack the eggs into the mixing bowl, one at a time; add the vanilla and lemon zest and continue to mix until fully combined. 6. Pour the prepared topping over the cooled crust and spread evenly. 7. Bake in the preheated air fryer at 164ºC for 25 to 30 minutes; leave it in the air fryer to keep warm for another 30 minutes. 8. Cover your cheesecake with plastic wrap. Place in your refrigerator and allow it to cool at least 6 hours or overnight. Serve well chilled.

Lime Bars

Prep time: 10 minutes | Cook time: 33 minutes |
Makes 12 bars

140 g blanched finely ground almond flour, divided	4 tablespoons salted butter, melted
75 g powdered sweetener, divided	120 ml fresh lime juice
	2 large eggs, whisked

1. In a medium bowl, mix together 110 g flour, 25 g sweetener, and butter. Press mixture into bottom of an ungreased round nonstick cake pan. 2. Place pan into air fryer basket. Adjust the temperature to 148ºC and bake for 13 minutes. Crust will be brown and set in the middle when done. 3. Allow to cool in pan 10 minutes. 4. In a medium bowl, combine remaining flour, remaining sweetener, lime juice, and eggs. Pour mixture over cooled crust and return to air fryer for 20 minutes. Top will be browned and firm when done. 5. Let cool completely in pan, about 30 minutes, then chill covered in the refrigerator 1 hour. Serve chilled.

Cardamom Custard

Prep time: 10 minutes | Cook time: 25 minutes | Serves 2

240 ml whole milk	¼ teaspoon vanilla bean paste
1 large egg	or pure vanilla extract
2 tablespoons granulated sugar,	¼ teaspoon ground cardamom,
plus 1 teaspoon	plus more for sprinkling

1. In a medium bowl, beat together the milk, egg, sugar, vanilla, and cardamom. 2. Place two ramekins in the air fryer basket. Divide the mixture between the ramekins. Sprinkle lightly with cardamom. Cover each ramekin tightly with aluminum foil. Set the air fryer to 176°C and cook for 25 minutes, or until a toothpick inserted in the center comes out clean. 3. Let the custards cool on a wire rack for 5 to 10 minutes. 4. Serve warm or refrigerate until cold and serve chilled.

Mini Peanut Butter Tarts

Prep time: 25 minutes | Cook time: 12 to 15 minutes | Serves 8

125 g pecans	cheese
110 g finely ground blanched	110 g cream cheese
almond flour	140 g sugar-free peanut butter
2 tablespoons unsalted butter, at	1 teaspoon pure vanilla extract
room temperature	⅛ teaspoon sea salt
50 g powdered sweetener, plus	85 g organic chocolate chips
2 tablespoons, divided	1 tablespoon coconut oil
120 g heavy (whipping) cream	40 g chopped peanuts or pecans
2 tablespoons mascarpone	

1. Place the pecans in the bowl of a food processor; process until they are finely ground. 2. Transfer the ground pecans to a medium bowl and stir in the almond flour. Add the butter and 2 tablespoons of sweetener and stir until the mixture becomes wet and crumbly. 3. Divide the mixture among 8 silicone muffin cups, pressing the crust firmly with your fingers into the bottom and part way up the sides of each cup. 4. Arrange the muffin cups in the air fryer basket, working in batches if necessary. Set the air fryer to 148°C and bake for 12 to 15 minutes, until the crusts begin to brown. Remove the cups from the air fryer and set them aside to cool. 5. In the bowl of a stand mixer, combine the heavy cream and mascarpone cheese. Beat until peaks form. Transfer to a large bowl. 6. In the same stand mixer bowl, combine the cream cheese, peanut butter, remaining 50 g sweetener, vanilla, and salt. Beat at medium-high speed until smooth. 7. Reduce the speed to low and add the heavy cream mixture back a spoonful at a time, beating after each addition. 8. Spoon the peanut butter mixture over the crusts and freeze the tarts for 30 minutes. 9. Place the chocolate chips and coconut oil in the top of a double boiler over high heat. Stir until melted, then remove from the heat. 10. Drizzle the melted chocolate over the peanut butter tarts. Top with the chopped nuts and freeze the tarts for another 15 minutes, until set. 11. Store the peanut butter tarts in an airtight container in the refrigerator for up to 1 week or in the freezer for up to 1 month.

Pecan Butter Cookies

Prep time: 5 minutes | Cook time: 24 minutes | Makes 12 cookies

125 g chopped pecans	150 g granulated sweetener,
110 g salted butter, melted	divided
55 g coconut flour	1 teaspoon vanilla extract

1. In a food processor, blend together pecans, butter, flour, 100 g sweetener, and vanilla 1 minute until a dough forms. 2. Form dough into twelve individual cookie balls, about 1 tablespoon each. 3. Cut three pieces of baking paper to fit air fryer basket. Place four cookies on each ungreased baking paper and place one piece baking paper with cookies into air fryer basket. Adjust air fryer temperature to 164°C and set the timer for 8 minutes. Repeat cooking with remaining batches. 4. When the timer goes off, allow cookies to cool 5 minutes on a large serving plate until cool enough to handle. While still warm, dust cookies with remaining granulated sweetener. Allow to cool completely, about 15 minutes, before serving.

5-Ingredient Brownies

Prep time: 10 minutes | Cook time: 25 minutes | Serves 6

Vegetable oil	3 large eggs
110 g unsalted butter	100 g granulated sugar
½ cup chocolate chips	1 teaspoon pure vanilla extract

1. Generously grease a baking pan with vegetable oil. 2. In a microwave-safe bowl, combine the butter and chocolate chips. Microwave on high for 1 minute. Stir very well. (You want the heat from the butter and chocolate to melt the remaining clumps. If you microwave until everything melts, the chocolate will be overcooked. If necessary, microwave for an additional 10 seconds, but stir well before you try that.) 3. In a medium bowl, combine the eggs, sugar, and vanilla. Whisk until light and frothy. Whisking continuously, slowly pour in the melted chocolate in a thin stream and whisk until everything is incorporated. 4. Pour the batter into the prepared pan. Set the pan in the air fryer basket. Set the air fryer to 176°C, and bake for 25 minutes, or until a toothpick inserted into the center comes out clean. 5. Let cool in the pan on a wire rack for 30 minutes before cutting into squares.

Pumpkin Pudding with Vanilla Wafers

Prep time: 10 minutes | Cook time: 12 to 17 minutes | Serves 4

250 g canned no-salt-added pumpkin purée (not pumpkin pie filling)
50 g packed brown sugar
3 tablespoons plain flour
1 egg, whisked
2 tablespoons milk
1 tablespoon unsalted butter, melted
1 teaspoon pure vanilla extract
4 low-fat vanilla, or plain wafers, crumbled
Nonstick cooking spray

1. Preheat the air fryer to 176°C. Coat a baking pan with nonstick cooking spray. Set aside. 2. Mix the pumpkin purée, brown sugar, flour, whisked egg, milk, melted butter, and vanilla in a medium bowl and whisk to combine. Transfer the mixture to the baking pan. 3. Place the baking pan in the air fryer basket and bake for 12 to 17 minutes until set. 4. Remove the pudding from the basket to a wire rack to cool. 5. Divide the pudding into four bowls and serve with the vanilla wafers sprinkled on top.

Orange Gooey Butter Cake

Prep time: 5 minutes | Cook time: 1 hour 25 minutes | Serves 6 to 8

Crust Layer:
60 g plain flour
50 g granulated sugar
½ teaspoon baking powder
⅛ teaspoon salt
60 g unsalted butter, melted
1 egg
1 teaspoon orange extract
2 tablespoons orange zest
Gooey Butter Layer:
230 g cream cheese, softened
110 g unsalted butter, melted
2 eggs
2 teaspoons orange extract
2 tablespoons orange zest
480 g icing sugar
Garnish:
Icing sugar
Orange slices

1. Preheat the air fryer to 176°C. 2. Grease a cake pan and line the bottom with baking paper. Combine the flour, sugar, baking powder and salt in a bowl. Add the melted butter, egg, orange extract and orange zest. Mix well and press this mixture into the bottom of the greased cake pan. Lower the pan into the basket using an aluminum foil sling (fold a piece of aluminum foil into a strip about 2-inches wide by 24-inches long). Fold the ends of the aluminum foil over the top of the dish before returning the basket to the air fryer. Air fry uncovered for 8 minutes. 3. Make the gooey butter layer: Beat the cream cheese, melted butter, eggs, orange extract and orange zest in a large bowl using an electric hand mixer. Add the icing sugar in stages, beat until smooth with each addition. Pour this mixture on top of the baked crust in the cake pan. Wrap the pan with a piece of greased aluminum foil, tenting the top of the foil to leave a little room for the cake to rise. 4. Air fry for 60 minutes. Remove the aluminum foil and air fry for an additional 17 minutes. 5. Let the cake cool inside the pan for at least 10 minutes. Then, run a butter knife around the cake and let the cake cool completely in the pan. When cooled, run the butter knife around the edges of the cake again and invert it onto a plate and then back onto a serving platter. Sprinkle the icing sugar over the top of the cake and garnish with orange slices.

Glazed Cherry Turnovers

Prep time: 10 minutes | Cook time: 14 minutes per batch | Serves 8

2 sheets frozen puff pastry, thawed
600 g can premium cherry pie filling
2 teaspoons ground cinnamon
1 egg, beaten
90 g sliced almonds
120 g icing sugar
2 tablespoons milk

1. Roll a sheet of puff pastry out into a square that is approximately 10-inches by 10-inches. Cut this large square into quarters. 2. Mix the cherry pie filling and cinnamon together in a bowl. Spoon ¼ cup of the cherry filling into the center of each puff pastry square. Brush the perimeter of the pastry square with the egg wash. Fold one corner of the puff pastry over the cherry pie filling towards the opposite corner, forming a triangle. Seal the two edges of the pastry together with the tip of a fork, making a design with the tines. Brush the top of the turnovers with the egg wash and sprinkle sliced almonds over each one. Repeat these steps with the second sheet of puff pastry. You should have eight turnovers at the end. 3. Preheat the air fryer to 188°C. 4. Air fry two turnovers at a time for 14 minutes, carefully turning them over halfway through the cooking time. 5. While the turnovers are cooking, make the glaze by whisking the icing sugar and milk together in a small bowl until smooth. Let the glaze sit for a minute so the sugar can absorb the milk. If the consistency is still too thick to drizzle, add a little more milk, a drop at a time, and stir until smooth. 6. Let the cooked cherry turnovers sit for at least 10 minutes. Then drizzle the glaze over each turnover in a zigzag motion. Serve warm or at room temperature.

Chapter 9 Staples, Sauces, Dips, and Dressings

Cashew Mayo

Prep time: 5 minutes | Cook time: 0 minutes | Makes 18 tablespoons

235 ml cashews, soaked in hot water for at least 1 hour
60 ml plus 3 tablespoons milk
1 tablespoon apple cider vinegar
1 tablespoon freshly squeezed

lemon juice
1 tablespoon Dijon mustard
1 tablespoon aquafaba or egg alternative
⅛ teaspoon pink Himalayan salt

In a food processor, combine all the ingredients and blend until creamy and smooth.

Homemade Remoulade Sauce

Prep time: 5 minutes | Cook time: 0 minutes | Serves 4

180 ml mayonnaise
1 garlic clove, minced
2 tablespoons mustard
1 teaspoon horseradish

1 teaspoon Cajun seasoning
1 teaspoon dill pickle juice
½ teaspoon paprika
¼ teaspoon hot pepper sauce

Whisk together all the ingredients in a small bowl until completely mixed. It can be used as a delicious dip for veggies, a sandwich or burger spread, or you can serve it with chicken fingers for a dipping sauce.

Tzatziki

Prep time: 10 minutes | Cook time: 0 minutes | Serves 4

1 large cucumber, peeled and grated (about 475 ml)
235 ml plain Greek yoghurt
2 to 3 garlic cloves, minced
1 tablespoon tahini (sesame

paste)
1 tablespoon fresh lemon juice
½ teaspoon rock salt, or to taste
Chopped fresh parsley or dill, for garnish (optional)

In a medium bowl, combine the cucumber, yoghurt, garlic, tahini, lemon juice, and salt. Stir until well combined. Cover and chill until ready to serve. Right before serving, sprinkle with chopped fresh parsley, if desired.

Italian Dressing

Prep time: 5 minutes | Cook time: 0 minutes | Serves 12

60 ml red wine vinegar
120 ml extra-virgin olive oil
¼ teaspoon salt
¼ teaspoon freshly ground black pepper

1 teaspoon dried Italian seasoning
1 teaspoon Dijon mustard
1 garlic clove, minced

In a small jar, combine the vinegar, olive oil, salt, pepper, Italian seasoning, mustard, and garlic. Close with a tight-fitting lid and shake vigorously for 1 minute. Refrigerate for up to 1 week.

Sweet Ginger Teriyaki Sauce

Prep time: 5 minutes | Cook time: 0 minutes | Serves 4

60 ml pineapple juice
60 ml low-salt soy sauce
2 tablespoons packed brown sugar

1 tablespoon arrowroot powder or cornflour
1 tablespoon grated fresh ginger
1 teaspoon garlic powder

Mix together all the ingredients in a small bowl and whisk to incorporate. Serve immediately, or transfer to an airtight container and refrigerate until ready to use.

Peanut Sauce with black pepper

Prep time: 5 minutes | Cook time: 0 minutes | Serves 4

80 ml peanut butter
60 ml hot water
2 tablespoons soy sauce
2 tablespoons rice vinegar

Juice of 1 lime
1 teaspoon minced fresh ginger
1 teaspoon minced garlic
1 teaspoon black pepper

In a blender container, combine the peanut butter, hot water, soy sauce, vinegar, lime juice, ginger, garlic, and pepper. Blend until smooth. Use immediately or store in an airtight container in the refrigerator for a week or more.

Dijon and Balsamic Vinaigrette

Prep time: 5 minutes | Cook time: 0 minutes | Makes 12 tablespoons

6 tablespoons water
4 tablespoons Dijon mustard
4 tablespoons balsamic vinegar
1 teaspoon maple syrup

½ teaspoon pink Himalayan salt
¼ teaspoon freshly ground black pepper

In a bowl, whisk together all the ingredients.

Mushroom Apple Gravy

Prep time: 5 minutes | Cook time: 10 minutes | Serves 4

475 ml vegetable broth
120 ml finely chopped mushrooms
2 tablespoons wholemeal flour
1 tablespoon unsweetened apple sauce

1 teaspoon onion powder
½ teaspoon dried thyme
¼ teaspoon dried rosemary
⅛ teaspoon pink Himalayan salt
Freshly ground black pepper, to taste

In a non-stick saucepan over medium-high heat, combine all the ingredients and mix well. Bring to a boil, stirring frequently, reduce the heat to low, and simmer, stirring constantly, until it thickens.

Green Basil Dressing

Prep time: 10 minutes | Cook time: 0 minutes | Makes 235 ml

1 avocado, peeled and pitted
60 ml sour cream
60 ml extra-virgin olive oil
60 ml chopped fresh basil
1 tablespoon freshly squeezed

lime juice
1 teaspoon minced garlic
Sea salt and freshly ground black pepper, to taste

Place the avocado, sour cream, olive oil, basil, lime juice, and garlic in a food processor and pulse until smooth, scraping down the sides of the bowl once during processing. Season the dressing with salt and pepper. Keep the dressing in an airtight container in the refrigerator for 1 to 2 weeks.

Lemony Tahini

Prep time: 5 minutes | Cook time: 0 minutes | Serves 4

180 ml water
120 ml tahini
3 garlic cloves, minced

Juice of 3 lemons
½ teaspoon pink Himalayan salt

In a bowl, whisk together all the ingredients until mixed well.

Traditional Caesar Dressing

Prep time: 10 minutes | Cook time: 5 minutes | Makes 350 ml

2 teaspoons minced garlic
4 large egg yolks
60 ml wine vinegar
½ teaspoon mustard powder
Dash Worcestershire sauce

235 ml extra-virgin olive oil
60 ml freshly squeezed lemon juice
Sea salt and freshly ground black pepper, to taste

To a small saucepan, add the garlic, egg yolks, vinegar, mustard, and Worcestershire sauce and place over low heat. Whisking constantly, cook the mixture until it thickens and is a little bubbly, about 5 minutes. Remove saucepan from the heat and let it stand for about 10 minutes to cool. Transfer the egg mixture to a large stainless-steel bowl. Whisking constantly, add the olive oil in a thin stream. Whisk in the lemon juice and season the dressing with salt and pepper. Transfer the dressing to an airtight container and keep in the refrigerator for up to 3 days.

Air Fryer Avocado Dressing

Prep time: 5 minutes | Cook time: 0 minutes | Makes 12 tablespoons

1 large avocado, pitted and peeled
120 ml water
2 tablespoons tahini
2 tablespoons freshly squeezed lemon juice

1 teaspoon dried basil
1 teaspoon white wine vinegar
1 garlic clove
¼ teaspoon pink Himalayan salt
¼ teaspoon freshly ground black pepper

Combine all the ingredients in a food processor and blend until smooth.

Lemon Cashew Dip

Prep time: 10 minutes | Cook time: 0 minutes | Makes 235 ml

180 ml cashews, soaked in water for at least 4 hours and drained
Juice and zest of 1 lemon
60 ml water

2 tablespoons chopped fresh dill
¼ teaspoon salt, plus additional as needed

Blend the cashew, lemon juice and zest, and water in a blender until smooth and creamy. Fold in the dill and salt and blend again. Taste and add additional salt as needed. Transfer to the refrigerator to chill for at least 1 hour to blend the flavours. This dip perfectly goes with the crackers or tacos. It also can be used as a sauce for roasted vegetables, or a sandwich spread.

Hot Honey Mustard Dip

Prep time: 5 minutes | Cook time: 0 minutes | Makes 315 ml

180 ml mayonnaise

80 ml spicy brown mustard

60 ml honey

½ teaspoon cayenne pepper

In a medium bowl, stir together the mayonnaise, mustard, and honey until blended. Stir in the cayenne. Cover and chill for 3 hours so the flavours blend. Keep refrigerated in an airtight container for up to 3 weeks.

Pepper Sauce

Prep time: 10 minutes | Cook time: 20 minutes | Makes 1 L

2 red hot fresh chillies, seeded

2 dried chillies

½ small brown onion, roughly chopped

2 garlic cloves, peeled

475 ml water

475 ml white vinegar

In a medium saucepan, combine the fresh and dried chillies, onion, garlic, and water. Bring to a simmer and cook for 20 minutes, or until tender. Transfer to a food processor or blender. Add the vinegar and blend until smooth.

Printed in Great Britain
by Amazon

16376667R00047